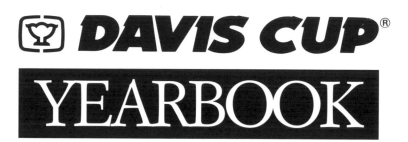

First published in the United States of America in 1996

by UNIVERSE PUBLISHING

A Division of Rizzoli International Publications, Inc.

300 Park Avenue South

New York, NY 10010

96 97 98 99 / 10 9 8 7 6 5 4 3 2 1

Design by Sam Serebin

Printed in Italy

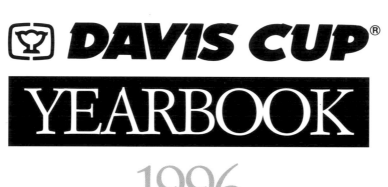

DAVIS CUP® YEARBOOK 1996

Text by Ronald Atkin

The International Tennis Federation

Universe

Contents:

Wimbledon's Court One in play for the last time during the Group II Euro/African Zone tie between Great Britain and Egypt

President's Message

It is my great pleasure to introduce the first Davis Cup Yearbook, a work which provides further proof, if any were needed, of the continuing expansion in popularity and interest in the world's premier annual sporting event.

In 1997, the number of competing nations has set another record with 127 countries involved. Yet, when the competition began in 1900, there were only two participating countries, the United States and the British Isles.

Now we are fast approaching the centenary of the Davis Cup, to be celebrated at the millenium. I am sure that, by then, the heartwarming expansion of tennis in the developing countries will have ensured yet another record number of entries.

That expansion and upsurge is reflected in the pictures and words on the pages of this book. It is a pictorial record of one of the world's truly great sporting competitions, a competition which enjoys the wholehearted support of the players, spectators, media and our loyal sponsors.

BRIAN TOBIN

President, International Tennis Federation

I am delighted to have been invited to provide the foreword for this book because I have always felt that being selected to represent your country is the greatest honour that can be bestowed on an athlete. I was only 18 when I was first chosen by Sweden to play in the Davis Cup and since that year, 1984, I have always been proud to play for my nation in a competition which is an integral, and essential, part of tennis.

I regard the Davis Cup as essential because tennis, especially professional tennis, is very much an individual sport. But when you are chosen to play Davis Cup you are part of a team fighting for your homeland in the world's greatest annual sporting competition.

The tennis circuit is such a busy one that players sometimes find it difficult, not to mention inconvenient, to fit Davis Cup calls into their schedule. You may be in the middle of a hard court season when you are required to fly halfway round the world to compete on clay. But the vast majority of tennis players are aware that such sacrifices are well worth making, and the rewards are immense.

I remember my debut very clearly. It was as a doubles player, partnered by Anders Jarryd, in the tie against Paraguay at Bastad in 1984. We lost that match to Victor Pecci and Francisco Gonzalez. I didn't play particularly well, but the team won 4–1. Then we beat Czechoslovakia 5–0 before facing, and overcoming, a powerful United States team in the Final. Jarryd and I played our part, defeating the world's top doubles pair, John McEnroe and Peter Fleming. That was such a great feeling, winning the Davis Cup the first year I had competed. Another great feeling was that our success brought tennis into many Swedish homes and helped boost the sport even more.

Since that first victory I have been privileged to be a regular member of the Swedish team. Eventually I became used to the demands of such occasions but I had to work hard to adapt to those demands. I was nervous on my debut in 1984 and I have to confess I was a little nervous, too, when I made my farewell to tennis by playing in my seventh Davis Cup Final against France in Malmö. And in my home country too!

I have been fortunate enough to enjoy much success in my dozen years on the circuit, and many of my most memorable moments came in the wonderful atmosphere which is unique to the Davis Cup. Long may it flourish.

When a twenty-year-old Harvard student, Dwight Filley Davis, of St. Louis, Missouri, offered a large silver punchbowl for international tennis competition in 1900, he could not, in his wildest dreams, have imagined what he was starting.

From that first year, when the only challengers to the United States were a team from the British Isles, the Davis Cup has grown into the world's biggest annual sporting event (the Olympics and soccer's World

Above: Malcolm Whitman, Dwight Filley Davis, Holcombe Ward; the winning USA team in 1900. **Right:** Dwight Filley Davis, founder of the competition

Cup are bigger but take place quadrennially). In 1997 there will be 127 nations involved in the various groups of the Davis Cup by NEC.

In that first year the United States, with Davis himself a member of the team, routed an under-strength British squad at Longwood, Boston, in a heat wave in which temperatures soared to 136 degrees Fahrenheit (57.8 centigrade). The following year, with the British unable to raise a squad, there was no competition but any fears that the Davis Cup might be a short-lived affair were unfounded. By the time of the First World War the two original nations had been joined by Australasia (Australia and New Zealand's combined team), Austria, Canada, Belgium, France and Germany.

However, until 1927 the only three nations to win the Cup were the United States (10 times), Australasia (6) and the British Isles (5). Then came the swashbuckling era of France's "Four Musketeers"—Jean Borotra, Rene Lacoste, Henri Cochet and Jacques Brugnon—when the trophy was claimed by the French six years in succession.

Borotra recalled subsequently that those times of triumph provided "a wonderful unity of spirit" in the French team. Many others who have represented their countries have said essentially the same, that playing in the Davis Cup has been among the greatest thrills of their careers.

Great Britain were next to dominate, capturing the Davis Cup from

France in Paris in 1933 and holding it until beaten by the United States at Wimbledon in 1937.

After the Second World War the trophy was dominated for 28 years by the United States and Australia. The Australians won on 16 occasions, the Americans 12. For 18 of those years those two nations contested the final, but after the scrapping of the Challenge Round in 1972 and the inexorable broadening of competition and improvement of European countries, it became a much more open affair.

The Challenge Round format had decreed that the country which won the trophy in the previous year was not required to defend it until the final against the winner of an elimination involving the other entrants.

This was a procedure as manifestly old-fashioned as the banning of professional players, which had not been lifted until the advent of open tennis in 1968. Since then, it has been wonderful, open, thrilling competition all the way. The United States hold the record for most wins with 31 victories and Australia are next with 26. Nobody else has managed double figures, but since the abolition of the Challenge Round and the introduction of the World Group there have been eight different champion nations.

The Davis Cup promotes a wonderful loyalty and pride. It has involved players as young as 14 and as old as 48. Italy's Nicola Pietrangeli played 164 matches in 66 ties and Ilie Nastase of Romania was not far behind with 146 matches in 62 ties.

Nobody has better articulated the Davis Cup's enduring attraction than the late Arthur Ashe, who both played for and captained the United States. In 1977 he wrote, "The Davis Cup endures as few other institutions have done before it. The Davis Cup is not a place or a player, a cup or a contest, a name or a notion. It is an idea, and it will always be just that. Furthermore, it is not an accident that the word ideal is derived from the word idea. Dwight Davis must have been an idealist when in 1900 he went to the trouble of donating the huge silver bowl, a symbol of friendly tennis rivalry. . . . The Davis Cup rules have changed, political systems have changed, even the cup itself has changed, but the idea and its ideals are immutable."

Right: Dwight Davis practises before the inaugural tie between the United States and the British Isles in Boston.

Introduction

It was, as everyone lucky enough to be present recognised, a very special occasion. An occasion to savour and relish, an historic occasion. The most astonishing finale to a Davis Cup Final in the competition's 96-year history. France's 3–2 victory over Sweden in Malmö was all this and more, a last-day marathon of more than nine hours of cliffhanging tennis that left spectators drained, winners jubilant, losers in tears.

Sweden versus France was the longest and closest Davis Cup Final ever. These occasions do not often go the full distance. Indeed, the last time the fifth rubber of a Final was relevant to the result was back in 1985. But Malmö 1996 had the lot. As Sweden's captain, Carl-Axel

Cedric Pioline (above) and Stefan Edberg (right) go for backhand shots. Following pages: Arnaud Boetsch's clenched fist indicates a point gained. Thomas Enqvist takes to the air to strike a forehand.

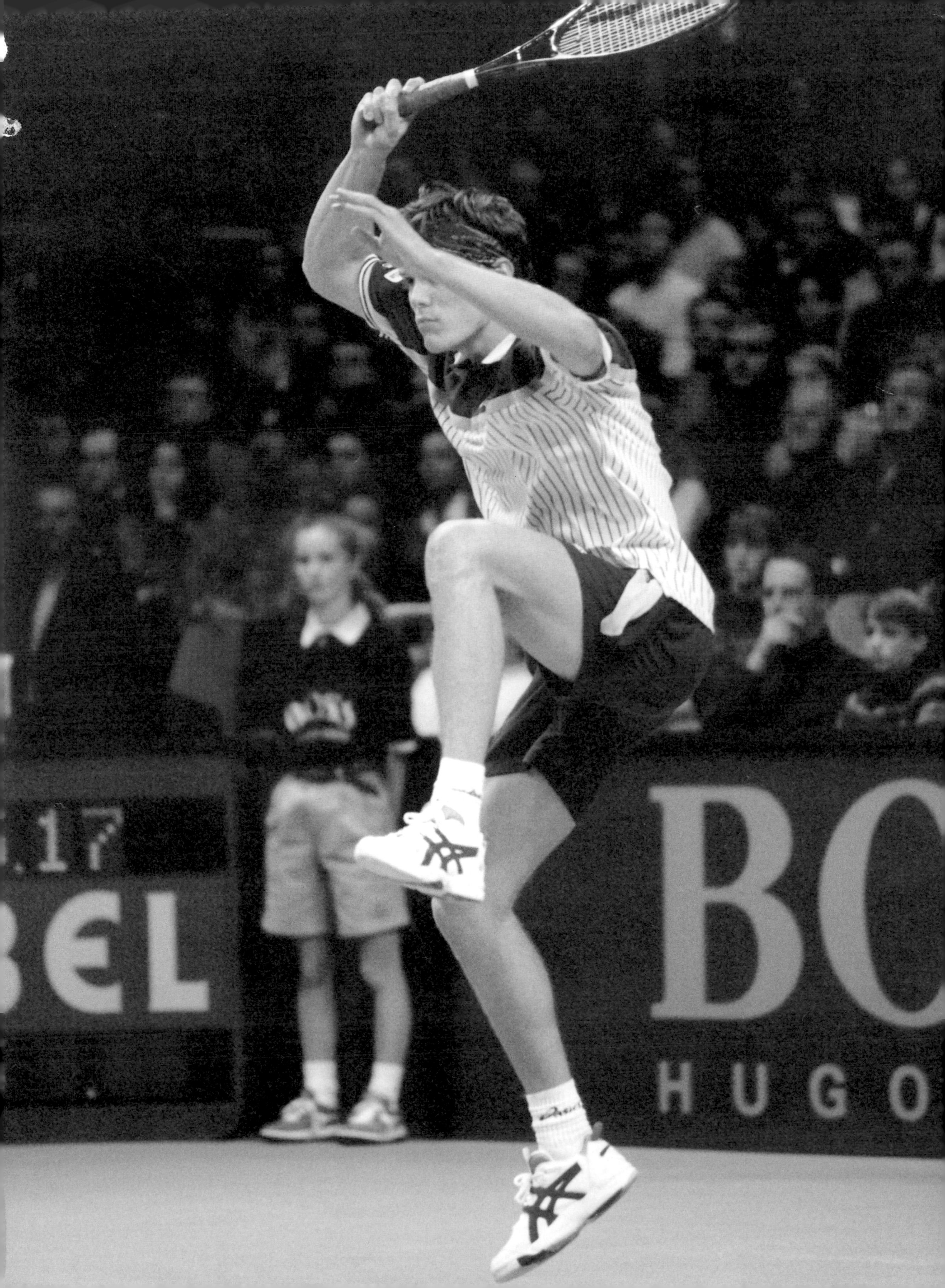
17
BEL
BO
HUGO

Hageskog, said, "I don't think Alfred Hitchcock could have done this better."

Sweden had gone into the last day trailing 2–1 and knowing that Stefan Edberg, whose final appearance of a long farewell year this was, would be unfit to play because of a damaged right ankle. Nicklas Kulti was the replacement for Edberg in the fifth and final rubber of the tie, but first Thomas Enqvist had to keep Sweden alive by beating Cedric Pioline. This he did, in five sets and four hours 25 minutes, in a marvellous contest played out before a packed house of 4,500 totally involved supporters, Swedish and French.

So Kulti was thrown in at the deep end against the more experienced and higher-ranked Arnaud Boetsch and no one could have complained if he had sunk without trace. Instead he battled and

Nicklas Kulti (left) chases a shot to his backhand while Cedric Pioline (above) commiserates with his beaten and injured opponent, Stefan Edberg.

came agonisingly close to overthrowing his
opponent and bringing the Davis Cup to
Sweden for a sixth time. Three match
points were Kulti's for the taking in the
fifth set but he was too hobbled by cramp
to profit. So, when an overjoyed Boetsch
finally put the sword to his crippled adver-
sary after four hours 47 minutes, France
were champions for the eighth time.

**The moment of glory for France as Arnaud
Boetsch discards his racket after the Cup-
winning point (above) and is then em-
braced by Guillaume Raoux (right)**

The last one had been 1991, against
the United States in Lyon, and Yannick
Noah had been France's captain then
too. Now the inspirational Noah articulated for everyone—not just the French,
but everyone—just what this astonishing
Davis Cup Final had meant. After lifting
Edberg onto his shoulders, after refusing
his champions' medal so that the French
team's hitting partner, Lionel Roux,
could be given the award instead, Noah

**Nicklas Kulti (above) surprised the
French by his strength and determination
but the victors were swift to honour the
vanquished (right). Following pages: All
together now... the entire French squad
form a circle to celebrate their nation's
eighth Davis Cup success.**

praised "this most beautiful occasion," adding, "it was the most wonderful Davis Cup tie of my life. I never thought a last day could go that far, with so much emotion, great tennis, unbelievable atmosphere and then the last match going to the fifth set. We were in the middle of something special, another dimension. I feel very privileged that I was there to experience it. The only pity was that the whole thing couldn't have ended in a tie."

All but the most rabid French followers would have agreed with that. As Swedish captain Hageskog said sadly, "Sometimes sport is very cruel."

But it is also sometimes very beautiful. Malmö in the Swedish snows of December brought to a stunning close a vibrant year for a very special sporting competition, the Davis Cup by NEC.

Yannick Noah exercises a captain's prerogative in embracing his victorious doubles player Guillaume Raoux (left) and later enjoys a brief quiet interlude (above) with his replica of the trophy. Following pages: The winners and their reward...pictured with the Davis Cup are Cedric Pioline, Arnaud Boetsch, Lionel Roux, Yannick Noah, Guy Forget and Guillaume Raoux.

Russia

Italy

Austria

South Africa

Denmark

France

Switzerland

Germany

Belgium

Sweden

Netherlands

India

Hungary

Czech Republic

Mexico

United States

First Round

It all began on the perfect, sunny morning of 8 January in Nairobi, Kenya, as 14 nations set out to do battle before a modest crowd in Zone B of the Euro/African Group III. Only four weeks earlier, the victorious Americans had grouped around the vast Davis Cup trophy inside the Moscow Olympic Hall after defeating Russia in the 1995 final. Now the 1996 competition was under way, with a record total of 124 countries in the world's biggest annual sporting event. It could hardly have been a more modest start; Kenya, the host nation, faced Botswana, while other countries in action were Bulgaria, Cameroon, Congo, Cyprus, Djibouti, Estonia, Greece, Ireland, Moldova, Monaco, Togo, and Zambia.

When the Nairobi occasion ended seven days later, Ireland and Greece had best survived the demands of slippery clay courts and secured promotion to Group II of the Euro/African Zone in 1997.

Another month was to pass before the vast majority of the competing nations, including the 16-strong World Group, went into action. Then, in the aftermath of the Ford Australian Open in Melbourne, the first of the year's Grand Slam tournaments, the biggest names and the most powerful nations began their bid to become the champions. There were the familiar heavyweights—the United States, Germany, Sweden; previous winners like the Czech Republic, France and South Africa; and lesser lights such as Mexico, Belgium, Denmark and Hungary, who had battled through the World Group qualifying round the previous autumn.

The draw had been kind to the United States, the 1995 champions, but cruel to Russia, the runners-up. The Americans had a home tie with Mexico, back in the World Group for the first time since 1991. Mexico's chances of staying at the top level of the competition were bleak; the two countries had met in previous Davis Cups thirty times and the Mexicans emerged as winners on only three occasions. Yet Mexico had edged past Spain, one of the world's best-equipped clay court nations, in the qualifying round,

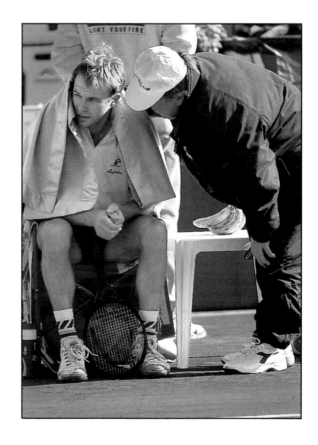

Left: Brett Steven led the Kiwi charge in New Zealand's 4–1 defeat of China in Asia/Oceania Zone Group I. **Below:** Russia's Yevgeny Kafelnikov gets a blanket and advice on how to keep warm on a chilly and depressing day against Italy in Rome.

Above: Oscar Ortiz strikes a forehand—but in a losing cause for Mexico. **Right:** Todd Martin, who said he would be available for play for his country "any place, any time," was a stalwart in the victory over Mexico.

so could not be regarded too lightly by the champions.

With a quintet like Andre Agassi, Michael Chang, Jim Courier, Todd Martin and Pete Sampras to choose their singles players from, the strength of the United States was formidable. Sampras, however, was of the opinion that his Moscow heroics in the December final were enough of a commitment for the time being. Agassi declared himself unavailable for Davis Cup all year; nor was Courier available. So Chang and Martin more or less selected themselves for the American captain, Tom Gullikson, while the two Patricks, Galbraith and McEnroe, formed the doubles team.

With the expectation of giving attendance a lift, the tie was staged at the La Costa Resort, in Carlsbad, California, forty miles from the Mexican border—only a few miles, in fact, from Tijuana, the home town of the eighteen-year-old Alejandro Hernandez, a surprise singles selection by Mexico's captain, Raul Ramirez. The site was criticised by Martin as a mistake. "We don't feel like it's a home tie when it's the visiting team making all the noise," he said. However, the loud support of Mexico's followers was of little assistance to their players.

Chang, playing Davis Cup by NEC for the first time in six years, got the United States away to a glorious start. He dropped only three points on serve in a first set that lasted a mere twenty-one minutes before going on to crush Leonard Lavalle 6–1 6–2 6–4. Martin was even less generous against Hernandez, conceding only six games in another straight-sets victory. The winning margin was secured the next day by the inexperienced American combination of Galbraith and McEnroe, who had not played together since 1992. It was also only McEnroe's third Davis Cup tie, and Galbraith's first. Yet, after overcoming a tiebreak in the opening set, they too ran away with a win in three sets against Lavalle and Oscar Ortiz. Mexico salvaged one set from the wreckage, and that was in the dead reverse singles when Lavalle went down 3–6 7–6 6–4 to Martin.

A similarly undemanding occasion, or even weather to match the eighty-degree temperatures of Carlsbad, would have suited the Russians, too. Instead, they

Michael Chang was in irrepressible form against Mexico, winning two singles rubbers for the loss of a mere thirteen games.

were required to travel to Italy, who possess a solid Davis Cup record, and to play outdoors in February on the clay courts of Rome's Foro Italico. It proved too much—just—for that old campaigner, Andrei Chesnokov, and the highly talented newcomer, Yevgeny Kafelnikov. Wearing a sweater and long trousers, and sipping hot drinks while wrapped in a blanket at the changeovers, Kafelnikov won both his singles, yet was unable to prevent a 3–2 Italian victory.

Having won the Davis Cup in 1976, finished runners-up five times, and never been out of the World Group since it was formed in 1981, Italy were clearly dangerous opposition for the 1995 finalists, even though their players were not quite of the calibre of former years. Andrea Gaudenzi got Italy off to a great start when he conjured victory from the brink of a straight-sets defeat against Chesnokov. Trailing by two sets and 4–1, Gaudenzi warmed the chilled fans by capturing the third set in a tiebreak and then dropping only four more games as he hustled to victory in four hours and eight minutes against an opponent who specialises in grinding out five-setters. It was only the second five-set match of Gaudenzi's career, and such were his high spirits that Italian captain Adriano Panatta caused a surprise by nominating him to play doubles with Diego Nargiso after Kafelnikov had levelled the tie at 1–1 by beating Renzo Furlan in four sets. The gamble worked magnificently, as the scratch Italian pairing, playing together for only the second time, defeated the experienced Russian duo of Kafelnikov and Andrei Olhovskiy in another tense five-set contest. Once again, Kafelnikov, who would go on to win the French Open less than four months later, stepped in to save his country by defeating Gaudenzi in the reverse singles to leave the tie poised at 2–2. Then, in the rain and gloom, Furlan showed more resolve and purpose than Chesnokov, winning 6–0 3– 6 6–3 7–5.

The weather was also a major factor in Johannesburg, where South Africa emerged victorious by a 3–2 margin over Austria in a tie that started on grass and was driven indoors by rain. In a bid to counter the slow-court strengths of Austria's number one, Thomas Muster, the South Africans marked out a grass court on the Wanderers Cricket Club ground. The strategy seemed to have misfired when

Muster opened the contest with a brisk 6–2 7–5 6–2 win over Marcos Ondruska, his first-ever victory on grass. Then misfortune struck the Austrians when their number two, Gilbert Schaller, was ruled out by a shoulder injury. His replacement, Wolfgang Schranz, ranked only 495 in the world, proved no match on this, his Davis Cup by NEC debut, for the top-rated South African, Wayne Ferreira.

In the doubles, a match played out over three days with rain providing frequent disruption, Ferreira and Gary Muller were leading Muster and Alex Antonitsch 6–3 7–6 6–7 1–2 when play was eventually moved onto the carpet surface of the Standard Bank Arena. The Austrians levelled the match by winning the fourth set 6–3, only for Ferreira and Muller to snatch the deciding set by a similar margin. Grass or carpet, it made no difference to Muster, who took over as world number one in the rankings during the hectic Johannesburg weekend. The rugged left-hander pulled off a stunning 7–5 6–7 6–4 7–6 victory over Ferreira, setting up the prospect of an upset win for Austria.

Yet this bizarre tie still had one more twist. Schranz, Schaller's replacement on the opening day, was himself taken ill, complaining of a stomach virus, and was unable to play the deciding rubber against Ondruska. So back came Schaller, now recovered from his injury, only to be beaten decisively, 6–3 6–4 6–2.

If Austria almost pulled off a surprise, India undoubtedly achieved a considerable upset by edging past the Netherlands 3–2 in Jaipur, to the delight of a boisterous, sell-out crowd. In this case, grass, the heat and an injury to Jacco Eltingh were the influencing factors, but nothing should be permitted to take away from the wonderful performance of the Indian team of Leander Paes and Mahesh Bhupathi, ranked 131 and 344 in the world, against two opponents ranked in the 20s and the other, Eltingh, ranked 71st.

Eltingh had set the Netherlands along the path to success with a straightforward 6–4 7–5 6–4 victory over Paes, who was crucially short of match practice at this sort of level. Then the twenty-one-year-old Bhupathi set about restoring

Left: Gambling on pairing Andrea Gaudenzi with Diego Nargiso in the doubles worked magnificently for Italy's captain, Adriano Panatta. **Below:** Wayne Ferreira's steadiness in both singles and doubles was crucial to South Africa's hopes.

India's fortunes against the world number 20, Jan Siemerink. He was leading 6–4 /–6 4–6 4–6 3–2 when bad light, followed by a dust storm, thunder and heavy rain forced an abandonment of play at the Jai Club. Although a disappointment to the spectators, the interruption proved a blessing to Bhupathi. Only recently recovered from a bout of flu, he was showing signs of tiredness in the fifth set after having already spent just under three hours on court.

Next morning, Bhupathi secured a service break in the tenth game and, after twenty minutes of play, had wrapped up the fifth set 6–4, and secured the most important win of his career, his first over five sets in the Davis Cup.

Once more, the Dutch appeared to have rescued themselves from trouble when Eltingh and Paul Haarhuis, the world's number two doubles pairing, beat Paes and Bhupathi 3–6 6–2 7–6 6–4 in two hours twenty-nine minutes. But the final day was one of unmitigated disaster for the visiting squad. First Paes, who so often reserves his best performances for the Davis Cup, upset Siemerink in a match of three tiebreaks, 7–6 2–6 7–6 7–6, despite having to overcome two penalty points awarded against India because of unruly behaviour by spectators, including shouting as Siemerink tossed up the ball to serve.

Having worked so hard to reach the brink of victory, India gained the stroke of luck that clinched success when Eltingh

Above: Jacco Eltingh's knee injury meant defeat for the Netherlands in Jaipur. **Right:** David Prinosil made a dream debut for Germany, winning both his singles rubbers.

twisted his knee in the opening set of the deciding singles rubber with Bhupathi. Though he played on into the fourth set, Eltingh was forced by the pain to retire with the score in India's favour, 7–6 4–6 7–5 2–1.

Germany, Davis Cup champions on three occasions since 1988, appeared to have a straightforward task when they were chosen to play Switzerland in Geneva. However, their squad was decimated when Boris Becker, who had just won the Australian Open, was forced out by inflamed leg ligaments, Marc-Kevin Goellner contracted flu and Michael Stich, still not fully recovered from a serious

Acrobatics from India's doubles team of Leander Paes and Mahesh Bhupathi helped to crush Dutch ambitions.

ankle injury, was only able to play doubles. Thus Germany were forced to offer Davis Cup debuts to twenty-two-year-old David Prinosil and twenty-one-year-old Hendrik Dreekmann against the highly-experienced Swiss combination of Marc Rosset, the Olympic champion, and Jakob Hlasek.

In the event, only the opening rubber, which went to five sets before Prinosil overcame Hlasek, proved a problem for the Germans as they romped to a marvellous 5–0 win. None of the other rubbers went beyond the minimum number of sets. So a nightmare build-up had become, for Germany, a fairy-tale conclusion. In mitigation for the Swiss, Rosset was woefully short of match practice after an appendicitis operation, and in the Hopman Cup in Perth over the new year, his only tournament since his return, he damaged his hand and was forced into another month's absence.

There were other, expected, 5–0 victories for France and the Czech Republic. They defeated two of the new arrivals in the World Group, Denmark and Hungary, respectively. Once again performing under the inspirational captaincy of Yannick Noah, who had led them to Davis Cup victory in 1991, the French enjoyed a romp in Besancon, the veteran left-hander

Above: So easy for Sweden . . . Magnus Larsson enjoys the success over Belgium. Right: Guy Forget demonstrates his commitment as France overwhelm Denmark.

Guy Forget setting his team on the victory route with a four-set win over Kenneth Carlsen. With fine support from Cedric Pioline in the singles and Guillaume Raoux in the doubles, Forget saw his side comfortably home by the end of the second day's play.

In Plzen, the Czechs were never in trouble against Hungary once Daniel Vacek and Petr Korda had demonstrated their singles superiority on the opening day, though the Hungarians extended the doubles rubber to five sets before conceding a winning margin to their hosts. The other tie in the World Group first round produced an easy win for Sweden, five-time Davis Cup champions, who beat Belgium 4–1 in Katrineholm. The Swedes had established a winning 3–0 margin without dropping a set before Johan van Herck salvaged some comfort for the Belgians by defeating Thomas Enqvist.

Russia

Italy

Austria

South Africa

Denmark

France

Switzerland

Germany

Belgium

Sweden

Netherlands

India

Hungary

Czech Republic

Mexico

United States

Quarter-Final Round

The United States's hold on the Davis Cup by NEC lasted exactly four months. Having beaten Russia in Moscow in December, the champions were defeated in April, in their second tie in defence of the trophy, when they went down 3–2 to the Czech Republic in Prague. The Americans paid a heavy price for the absence of their leading players in the early rounds of the 1996 event. Pete Sampras had promised to make himself available for the semi-final and final rounds later in the year, a gesture rendered superfluous by the Czechs' spirited performance. Andre Agassi and Jim Courier were again unavailable, and Michael Chang, who had won both his singles easily in the first round against Mexico, also declined to travel.

Above: Todd Martin's two impressive singles wins could not save the United States from defeat. **Right:** The talented but mercurial Petr Korda can determine the Davis Cup destiny of the Czech Republic.

So the United States pinned hopes of singles success on the ever-loyal Todd Martin, who had gone on record as saying he was available to play for his country "any place, any time," while the second singles berth was taken up by MaliVai Washington. For doubles, team captain Tom Gullikson again relied on Patrick Galbraith and Patrick McEnroe, the combination he had blooded against Mexico. It looked like an ominously thin squad with which to tackle a nation urgently seeking a place in the semi-finals for the first time in ten years, and so it proved.

Martin, however, was blameless, winning both his singles with the utmost comfort in straight sets. On the opening day, Martin, the world-ranked number 17, was masterful in his domination of a disappointing Petr Korda, who had struggled back up to 41st in the rankings after an injury kept him out for much of the 1995 season. Korda, with his coach Tony Pickard (former British Davis Cup captain and long-time coach of Stefan Edberg) sitting on the Czech team bench, did not get

into the match until he was two sets and a break down. Then, belatedly, he produced some of the fighting tennis for which he is famous in his home city of Prague, but too late. The home nation ended the opening day on level terms thanks to Daniel Vacek,

who defeated Washington in five grimly contested sets, 4–6 6–3 6–4 5–7 6–4. A defeat for Vacek in this rubber would almost certainly have ensured the United States a spot in the semi-finals.

Next day the Czech captain, Vladimir Savrda, made a late gamble for the doubles, picking his singles players, Korda and Vacek. The move was a spectacular success. Korda, so disappointing

the previous day, was inspirational, his returns skimming the net with such speed and accuracy that McEnroe found the volleying skills in which he specialises under severe pressure. It was also a measure of the Czechs' dominance on serve in their 6–2 6–3 6–3 win that only once did they have to fight off a break point.

The doubles, as is so often the case in a Davis Cup tie, turned out to be the crucial blow for the Czechs. As expected, Martin, reliable as ever, kept American hopes alive by overcoming Vacek 7–6 6–3 6–1, but in the deciding singles rubber, Washington was always struggling to bridge the gap in class between himself and Korda. He certainly made a fight of it in the first set; Korda had to fend off two set points before snatching Washington's serve on the opening point of the tiebreak and holding on to win it by seven points to five. After that, the Czech lefthander's elegant ground strokes and sizzling returns of serve proved too much for the American, who crumbled to a 7–6 6–3 6–3 defeat. With his sixth ace of the match, Korda sealed what was the Czechs' most enjoyable victory since the days when Ivan Lendl played for them.

Afterwards Gullikson refused to lay the blame for the shock loss on the absence

Above: Czech Republic's Daniel Vacek and Petr Korda proved an imposing tandem, winning the pivotal doubles match over the United States. Left: MaliVai Washington of the United States parried for five sets but lost against the powerful Daniel Vacek of Czech Republic.

Daniel Vacek won a grim, but crucial, five-setter for the Czech Republic against the United States.

of the top Americans or to make any excuses for losing. "They beat us on the tennis court, they played very well and they deserved to win," he said. "The players that we had here did their best and we can't really worry about who's not here."

A further reward for the Czech Republic was to be drawn at home, against Sweden in the semi-final. The Swedes, learning from the mistakes of the Netherlands team against India in the previous round, took every precaution against the heat for their quarter-final in Calcutta and were rewarded with a solid 5–0 victory. They prepared meticulously for long, exhausting matches and this paid off immediately when, in the opening rubber, Jonas Bjorkman lasted the pace better than Leander Paes in the one hundred-degree heat. It was the Indian player who suffered leg cramps as he lost 1–6 6–4 5–7 6–3 7–5 in a torrid three and a half hours. Then Sweden took firm control of the first day when Thomas Enqvist, the world's number nine rated player, overcame a nervous start to beat Mahesh Bhupathi, ranked 332 places below him and the hero of India's demolition of the Dutch. Once Enqvist had pulled level by winning the second tiebreak set of the match, Bhupathi's resolve melted.

Bjorkman, undefeated in Davis Cup doubles, kept his record intact when he teamed up with Nicklas Kulti to beat Paes and Bhupathi in four sets and send Sweden through to the semi-finals for the fifth straight year. The Indian pair won the first set on a tiebreak by seven points to four but the Swedes rallied so

Above: Lowly ranked Mahesh Bhupathi of India staged stunning upsets over the powerful Dutch team. **Left:** Jonas Bjorkman's acrobatics set Sweden an exhilarating example against India in Calcutta.

strongly that they annexed the next three sets at a cost of only eight games. The competitive nature of Paes showed when he battled Kulti all the way in a dead singles rubber; Kulti needed to serve sixteen aces to wrap up a 6–3 6–7 7–6 win before Bjorkman brushed aside Bhupathi in the second of the dead rubbers.

France, too, were in dominant form against Germany, recording an emphatic 5–0 win in Limoges to reach their first semi-final since the glory year of 1991. The Germans were again forced to pin their hopes in the singles on David Prinosil and Hendrik Dreekmann, heroes of the first round whitewash of Switzerland, since Michael Stich was out of action altogether, having undergone an operation on the ankle he had first damaged the previous autumn and Boris Becker, suffering the lingering effects of a respiratory ailment, was only able to play doubles.

France needed no invitation for their experienced campaigners to bear down on a German squad seriously undermanned for such an important occasion. Having gone off at a gallop by winning the first set to love against Prinosil, Cedric Pioline was subsequently given a much tougher fight. In a crucial third set, he was twice a break down before emerging a 6–0 6–7 6–4 6–3 winner. Arnaud Boetsch,

Above: A gloomy outlook . . . Boris Becker and his team captain Niki Pilic brace themselves for disaster against France. Right: Cedric Pioline's resilience set France on the road to a runaway success over Germany in Limoges.

France's number one, built on this lead with a dogged victory over Dreekmann in a marathon five-setter. Having played with much skill and courage early on, Dreekmann tired towards the end and was beaten 4–6 6–4 3–6 7–6 6–3.

Now Germany's hopes hung on Becker, their hero of so many Davis Cup battles. But he proved no more able to perform successfully in doubles than he might have in the singles. In harness with Marc-Kevin Goellner, Becker slid to a

Boris Becker, Germany's biggest gun, was firing blanks in the doubles with Marc-Kevin Goellner as they lost in straight sets to France.

7–6 6–4 7–6 defeat, sealing an unexpectedly straightforward win for France. It was France's third successive 5–0 win in the Davis Cup. "Fifteen rubbers without a defeat shows we have a really solid team," said the captain, Yannick Noah.

Another jubilant captain, Adriano Panatta, was given victory "bumps" by his delighted team after Italy's conclusive 4–1 win over South Africa on the clay of Rome's Foro Italico. There was probably a bit of relief in the Italians' attitude, since they had got off to a dreadful start when their number one, Renzo Furlan, slid to a shock 6–4 6–4 6–4 defeat against the South African second string, Marcos On-druska. A first day of solid accomplishment looked on the cards for South Africa, the 1974 Davis Cup champions. But Wayne Ferreira, their best player for many years, failed to take advantage of the inconsistencies of Andrea Gaudenzi and fell in five sets, losing the final set by a conclusive 6–1. The famed Foro Italico crowd did much to lift Gaudenzi to better things as Ferreira's game began to fall apart in the fourth set.

The next day's doubles also went to five sets as Gaudenzi and Diego Nargiso repeated their success of the previous round against Russia by defeating the Ferreiras, Wayne and Ellis (who are not related). Ellis, making his Davis Cup by NEC debut, failed to boost his namesake, who was having a disastrous time of it in Rome. Things got no better for Wayne when it came to play

the crucial reverse singles. Victory over Furlan was necessary for South Africa to stay in contention but, after a poor opening set, the Italian raised his game and Ferreira was unable to respond, falling to defeat in four sets, 3–6 6–0 7–6 6–2. A depressing tie from the South African point of view reached its nadir in the dead rubber when Ondruska was forced to retire with a foot injury when losing to Gaudenzi 6–1 1–1. After his "bumps," captain Panatta was understandably optimistic. "We have won a great match," he said. "Now let's move on to the semi-finals. It's a very open competition this year."

It was also, by this stage, an all-European competition after the quarter-final defeats suffered by the United States, India and South Africa. This was the first time Europe had filled all the semi-final places since 1988, when a Becker-inspired Germany scored their initial Davis Cup triumph. This time, however, Germany would not be in the last four. Yannnick Noah and his French team had seen to that.

In the Euro/African, American and Asia/Oceania Zone Group I competitions, the eight qualifiers for the World Group qualifying round for the

Above: Diego Nargiso and Andrea Gaudenzi's joy at their doubles win is matched by the jubilation of the Rome crowd. Right: A sharply judged backhand sends Renzo Furlan on the way to the deciding victory for Italy over South Africa.

1997 Davis Cup were decided. In the European Zone, Spain, Croatia and Morocco all had clear-cut wins over Israel, Ukraine and Zimbabwe respectively, while Romania just edged past Finland 3–2. Brazil and Argentina were winners in the American Zone. Brazil beat Venezuela 4–1 and Argentina defeated the Bahamas by the same margin. Australia and New Zealand were the qualifiers from the Asia/Oceania Zone. Australia cleaned up 5–0 against Japan in Ozaka, while New Zealand just prevailed by a score of 3–2 over Korea in Seoul.

Semi-Final Round

The Palais des Sports de Beaulieu in Nantes and Prague's Sportovni Hala were the indoor venues chosen by France and the Czech Republic for the tournament's semi-finals towards the end of September. Both were carefully selected, since home advantage in the draw offers the chance to nominate a preferred court surface and a location where home support can be maximised. Yet, initially, both site selections backfired. At the end of the opening day France trailed 2–0 to Italy and the Czechs were behind by a similar margin against Sweden. All eventually came right for the French in the most dramatic fashion, but there was no way that Sweden, with their experience of eight Davis Cup finals in twelve years between 1983 and 1994, would permit the Czechs to find a way back from those first-day disasters.

All week the nation of France had savoured the prospect of rolling over Italy and into the final. Everyone hoped it would be a repeat of the 1991 competition, in which the incomparable Yannick Noah and his inspired players tackled and brought to earth the might of the United States to win the trophy in Lyon.

Acres of newsprint and hours of television footage were devoted to France's preparations for this semi-final. "The French team is favourite," headlined *Le Monde*. Confidence was rampant to a dangerous degree, particularly after the discovery of a French gaffe in the matter of court selection. With the idea of nonplussing Italian opponents more accustomed to slow clay, the surface chosen was GreenSet Trophy, a synthetic rubberised court like the ones at the French Tennis Federation's training headquarters at Roland Garros.

What French officialdom and the team captain failed to anticipate was that GreenSet plays at one speed after several years of use and at quite another altogether—i.e. slow—

Above: Fears of impending disaster in the semi-final against Italy proved groundless for France's captain, Yannick Noah. **Right:** Italy's Andrea Gaudenzi in jubilant mood as he catches a glimpse of further progress for his country.

when new. The left-handed, big-serving Guy Forget, France's indoor ace, was horrified when he first practised on the newly-laid carpet. The state of the court drew a frank admission from Noah that he had, so to speak, taken his eye off the ball at a crucial moment: "I probably was not paying sufficient attention to what was being ordered."

The shock result when the French team was announced was that Forget had been left out of the singles. Many thought Noah should have played his most experienced Davis Cup by NEC campaigner, but the captain knows his man well. The tall, elegant Forget has been known to wobble in a crisis, and the slowness of the surface had been enough for a seed of doubt to be planted in his mind.

So Noah went with Arnaud Boetsch and Cedric Pioline as his singles choices against Andrea Gaudenzi and Renzo Furlan. The opening rubber saw the experienced 27-year-old Pioline, a runner-up at the U.S. Open only three years previously, drawn against Gaudenzi. The hall was packed to

its 4,500 person capacity and the French supporters whooped with delight as Pioline struck three aces in his first two service games. Perhaps the court would not prove so slow after all. Such hopes were reinforced as Gaudenzi fumbled away the opening set, committing three unforced errors on his serve to permit Pioline to take the twelfth game to love and go one set up.

Delight rapidly turned to dismay for the French fans as Pioline, dropping his serve and spraying errors all over the place, proceeded to lose ten of the next twelve games. A grateful Gaudenzi cruised to a 4–0 lead and not only pocketed the second set but went on to lead 4–1 in the third before Pioline managed to

Above: A pause for reflection as Arnaud Boetsch struggles to stay in contention in his singles against Renzo Furlan. **Left:** Andrea Gaudenzi stretches to strike a forehand in the Italy-France semi-final.

Above: Renzo Furlan strikes a winning blow for Italy on the first day of the semi-final against France. **Right:** Eyes on the prize . . . Arnaud Boetsch projects a backhand in the France-Italy semi-final.

apply the brakes to such an effect that he forced the set to a tiebreak. Then Pioline slipped again. With the score tied at three points all, the Frenchman struck a forehand wide. It was the crucial error as Gaudenzi closed out the tiebreak 7–4.

Although Gaudenzi damaged his left wrist making a spectacular dive in the opening game of the fourth set, it did nothing to dampen the Italian's exuberance and confidence, though his serving became as inept as Pioline's for a while. There were five breaks in the first seven games of what turned out to be the final set of this rubber until Gaudenzi finally held serve to go 5–3 up. Could Pioline find a way back even now? The feeble answer was a surrender of his serve for the ninth time in this three hour 11-minute match. Pioline had been beaten 5–7 6–1 7–6 6–3 in what he later called his worst-ever performance indoors. The 23-year-old Gaudenzi, wearing a headband in the national colours of red, white and green and nicknamed Monsieur Muscle by the French media, was the hero of the flag-flaunting Italian supporters. This had been by some distance the biggest Davis Cup singles victory of the 13 he had played in total.

Soon enough, the Italians had another hero to salute as Furlan, "The Italian Chang" according to *L'Equipe*, the French sports daily, dismantled Boetsch, also in four sets, by a score of 7–5 1–6 6–3 7–6. It was the manner as much as the fact of this defeat that left Noah numb at the end of a disastrous day for France. Despite leading 2–0 in the opening set, Boetsch contrived to offer Furlan the chance he sought by dropping serve in the eleventh game on a double fault and loose forehand, permitting the Italian to wrap it up in 51 minutes.

Boetsch's reaction was certainly a crowd-pleaser, as he ripped off the second set in a mere 37 minutes. But Furlan, happy to retrieve all day if offered the oppor-

tunity and also delighted by the slowness of this court, took the third set comfortably. Still, all was not lost for France. Boetsch held three break points on Italy's service twice in the fourth set. Both times, Furlan fought off looming disaster and at 5–4 served for the match. Boetsch battled back to take it to a tiebreak and the Tricolours were flaunted again as he surged to a five points to one lead. But Furlan, striking three passing shots of stunning skill, swept away French hopes by capturing six successive points to take the tiebreak, the match, and a 2–0 lead for his nation.

It took less than two hours on the second day for the faith of the chanting, klaxon-blowing French supporters to be restored. Their doubles combination of Forget and Guillaume Raoux needed only an hour and 57 minutes to overcome the Italians, Gaudenzi and Diego Nargiso, 6–3 6–4 6–2. The serve and volley expertise of Forget, ably abetted by Raoux's industry, was always too much for the Italians. The trend was established in the first set, which France captured in 32 minutes without facing a break point. Gaudenzi dropped serve in the eighth game, double-faulting twice, and when Nargiso did the same in the opening game of the second set, Italy were as good as out of it. Nargiso, who had expended considerable energy the previous day roaring on his compatriots from the team bench, perpetrated eight double faults.

Disappointing as the result—and their players' performance—had been, the Italians still needed only one victory from the final day's two singles rubbers to put them into a Davis Cup final for the first time since 1980. And the omens could hardly have been better since Gaudenzi, who was to play the final singles, had beaten Boetsch, his

Above: Arnaud Boetsch receives a victory hug from his captain, Yannick Noah, after his win over Italy's Andrea Gaudenzi secured a place in the final. Left: Arnaud Boetsch stretches for a running forehand on the way to the victory over Andrea Gaudenzi which put France into the final.

opponent, on both previous occasions they had met.

Before that, however, there was the contest between Pioline and Furlan, whose head-to-head record stood at one victory each. Pioline, ranked 17th in the world compared to Furlan's 38th ranking, served altogether better than he had done on Friday and wrapped up the first set 6–3 in 50 minutes. Back came Furlan to level the match by taking the second set 6–2 and there were anxious murmurs from French followers. These were soon stilled as Pioline opted for boldness as his best policy, moving to the net to put the pressure on his opponent and gaining reward with two breaks of serve in the third set to win it 6–2.

Furlan managed to save two break points in the first game of the fourth set, only for Pioline to break him in the third game, a moment that had Noah bounding to his feet in celebration. Serving for the match at 5–4, Pioline had three match points. Furlan

Above: His woes of the opening day forgotten, Cedric Pioline exults in the singles victory over Renzo Furlan which gave France a glimpse of a place in the final. **Right:** France's captain Yannick Noah and his backup squad enjoy the belated recovery against Italy.

saved the first with a dead net cord and Pioline missed the next when a backhand struck the tape. But at the third opportunity Pioline made no mistake, drilling an unstoppable ace down the middle and raising one finger in jubilation to the crowd, signaling to them that one more win was needed for the miracle to be complete.

Boetsch briskly set off in pursuit of that win, breaking serve in the opening game against Gaudenzi, whose left wrist was bandaged as a result of the spectacular tumble he had taken on the opening day. That break was enough to win the opening set for France in 47 minutes and, with Boetsch serving impeccably and an over-anxious Gaudenzi overhitting his returns, the second set for the home nation soon followed in 35 minutes.

When Gaudenzi was again broken in the first game of the third set it seemed all over. But in fact it was the beginning of a marvellous, see-saw third set. Gaudenzi

All of the skills and expertise acquired in 12 years of Davis Cup competition are on show as Stefan Edberg goes for a backhand.

broke back to 2–2, Boetsch immediately broke again for 3–2 and held on to lead 5–3. Gaudenzi held for 5–4 and then, as Boetsch's serve suddenly deserted him, levelled at 5–5 with a forehand pass as the Frenchman charged the net desperately. As Gaudenzi went in front 6–5 the Italian fans danced and cavorted in the stands, and there was more jubilation as Boetsch faced two set points in the next game. But he held on to take the set into a tiebreak and then moved to two match points, both of which were saved by the Italian, the first with a smash after a 22-stroke rally.

Twice more Gaudenzi saved match points before Boetsch struck a forehand winner to take the tiebreak by ten points to eight and the match 6–4 6–2 7–6. The

Right: The style is unorthodox but the intention crystal clear as Thomas Enqvist goes for a backhand winner. **Below:** A textbook backhand from Petr Korda could not stave off a straight-sets loss to Thomas Enqvist in the Prague semi-final.

French player dropped his racket in disbelief and only just remembered in time to shake hands with his bitterly disappointed opponent before being overwhelmed by the entire French team.

If the other semi-final in Prague did not offer such a momentous climax, it certainly contained much good tennis. On a fast indoor carpet, Sweden got off to an excellent start by winning both singles on the first day. Thomas Enqvist struck a mighty blow for his nation by crushing Petr Korda in straight sets 6–4 6–3 7–6. Korda certainly had his chances, particularly during the second set in which the Czech missed six break points. The third set was a wild affair, with both players dropping serve three times before Enqvist took the tiebreak by 11 points to nine.

Sweden could not have asked for a better man to ram home their advantage in the second singles than Stefan Edberg. Despite a late doubt about his fitness

because of lingering problems with an Achilles tendon injury sustained at the U.S. Open, Edberg declared himself fit to participate in his 34th Davis Cup tie. He proved too good for Czech number one Daniel Vacek, winning 7–6 7–5 4–6 6–3. His only stumble came when a service break cost him the third set.

The Swedes' plain sailing was disturbed only once; on the second day they were wrong-footed by the Czechs' late decision to switch their doubles team. The nominated pair of Jiri Novak and Bohdan Ulihrach was dropped and replaced by the singles players, Korda and Vacek. Not only was it a sensible decision since both men were current Grand Slam doubles champions (Korda with Edberg, of all people, at the Ford Australian Open and Vacek with Kafelnikov at Roland Garros) but it also turned out to be a winning gamble as they swept past Nicklas Kulti and Jonas Bjorkman 4–6 6–3 6–4 6–4. Afterwards Korda said, "We have not started out well but we are still alive."

Not for long, alas. On the final day, Enqvist, Sweden's hero, outlasted Vacek in a marathon five-setter, 6–3 6–7 4–6 7–5 6–3 in three hours, 18 minutes to ensure Sweden's tenth appearance in a Davis Cup by NEC final. Both men

are powerful servers but it was the quality of Enqvist's returns that tipped the balance in his favour. Enqvist's tendency to double-fault and a tactical decision by Vacek to slow down his game with sliced backhand returns saw the Czech take a two sets to one lead before he tired and faded. Perhaps the exertions of an unexpected outing in the doubles had drained his stamina. So Edberg, appearing in his final Davis Cup match abroad, played with the pressure off and duly beat Korda, his erstwhile doubles partner, in their best-of-three-sets dead rubber by 4–6 6–2 7–5.

Above: Thomas Enqvist receives the congratulations of his captain, Carl Axel Hageskog, after his five-set victory over Daniel Vacek in the Sweden-Czech Republic semi-final. **Left:** Stefan Edberg puts his mind to the task to seeing Sweden into another Davis Cup final.

Argentina

Mexico

Croatia

Australia

Austria

Brazil

Romania

Belgium

Netherlands

New Zealand

Hungary

Russia

Spain

Denmark

Morocco

Switzerland

**World Group
Qualifying Round**

The World Group Qualifying Round is always one of the most exciting segments of the Davis Cup by NEC year, with the eight first round losers in the premier section battling against eight zonal winners for the right to appear in the 1997 World Group of sixteen nations.

The winners were four of the nations that had been beaten in the first round back in February—Mexico, the Netherlands, Russia and Switzerland—together with four of the promoted zonal countries—Australia, Brazil, Romania and Spain. Perhaps the best wins were secured by Australia, who defeated Croatia 4–1 in Split, and Mexico, who made full use of their home advantage to beat Argentina 3–2.

However, the media glare was focused on the tie in São Paulo, where Austria refused to complete their doubles on the second day against Brazil and were subsequently defaulted. The tie was abandoned and awarded to Brazil by a score of 4–1. The two nations had gone into the second day's play level at 1–1. Thomas Muster defeated Fernando Meligeni in straight sets but the Austrian number two, the junior Markus Hipfl, making his debut in the competition, was beaten in five sets by Gustavo Kuerten de-

Above: Albert Costa unleashes a forehand as Spain head for comfortable victory over Denmark in the World Group Qualifying Round. **Right:** Thomas Muster and the Austrian captain, Ronnie Leitgeb, remonstrate with the umpire during their tie in São Paolo, Brazil.

spite having won the opening two sets. In the doubles, Kuerten and Jaime Oncins were leading Muster and Udo Plamberger 7–6 4–6 6–3 3–6 2–0 when Muster complained of being abused and intimidated by the crowd, alleging that someone in the stands was attempting to dazzle him with a mirror. In the opinion of the referee, Antonio Flores Marques of Portugal, the complaints were not justified and when Muster refused to play on, he was defaulted.

Under the Davis Cup Code of Conduct, Muster was then not eligible to play in the final day's singles rubbers. Austria declined to replace him with another team member and also declined to contest the two remaining singles. Two weeks later in London, the Davis Cup Committee ruled that the Austrian Tennis Association should forfeit their prize money of $58,760 for failing to complete the tie and that Muster should be fined $2,000 for verbal obscenity and a further $6,000 for leaving the court and refusing to play. So Brazil marched forward to the World Group draw for 1997 and immediately pulled out a plum in the shape of a home tie against the United States.

Australia's key victory in the 4–1 win over Croatia was secured by Jason Stoltenberg, who repeated his Wimbledon quarter-final defeat of the world number four and home

favourite Goran Ivanisevic, though this time he needed five sets instead of four. The victory was then sealed when the doubles team of Patrick Rafter and Mark Woodforde won in straight sets.

Mexico's hero in the tie with Argentina was Alejandro Hernandez, who won both his singles rubbers and teamed with Oscar Ortiz to capture the crucial doubles in five sets. Another excellent victory was secured by Romania over Belgium in a tie that went down to the last match before Andrei Pavel's success ensured a return for Romania to the World Group for the first time since 1984.

Even without the Wimbledon champion, Richard Krajicek, absent with a knee injury, and former world

Above: Andrea Pavel is entitled to celebrate as his second straight-sets win against Belgium puts Romania into the World Group for the first time since 1984. **Right:** Tim Henman of Great Britain strokes an elegant backhand in the Euro-African Zone Group II play-off against Egypt. The tie was the last competitive event to be played at Wimbledon's historic Court One before it was demolished.

doubles champions Jacco Eltingh and Paul Haarhuis, the Netherlands were too strong for New Zealand in Haarlem and won 4–1. Russia beat Hungary in Moscow by the same margin and Spain also marked a return to the top echelon of the competition with a 4–1 victory over Denmark in Tarragona, while Switzerland whitewashed Morocco.

The zonal ties produced one outstandingly nostalgic occasion when Britain opted to play their Euro/African Zone Group II Final Round against Egypt on Wimbledon's Court One. It was the last competitive match in this 72-year-old stadium before demolition workers prepared to move in as part of the All England Club's ground improvement scheme. Britain celebrated suitably by winning 5–0 and gaining promotion to Group I of the Euro/African Zone.

The stretch before the storm ... Thomas Muster goes for a backhand return in a World Group Qualifying tie which ended with Austria being defaulted against Brazil in São Paolo.

Adriano Panatta

In the 1996 Davis Cup the 46-year-old Adriano Panatta celebrated a momentous quarter-century of involvement with the competition. He made his debut as a player, aged 20, in a European Zone B tie against Czechoslovakia in Turin, losing in straight sets to Jan Kukal as Italy were beaten 3–2. Panatta played every year subsequently until 1984 when he was appointed captain, a position he has held ever since.

Panatta duelled with some of the greatest Davis Cup performers of all—Ilie Nastase, Bjorn Borg, John McEnroe—and was part of the Italian team in all four Davis Cup finals they contested between 1976 and 1980 (all of them played away from home, incidentally). In 1976, Italy defeated Chile 4–1 in Santiago, when Panatta won both his singles and also a doubles rubber. He played in the 1977 final against Australia in Sydney, which the Australians won 3–1, and in the 1979 final against the United States in San Francisco, when the U.S. won 5–0. In 1980, Czechoslovakia defeated Italy 4–1 in Prague.

Panatta stands sixteenth in the all-time Davis Cup win/loss records with a 64–36 record compiled in 38 ties. He won 37 singles and lost 26 and won 27 doubles and lost 10.

Left: The glory days for Italy's golden idol, Adriano Panatta, who celebrated a quarter-century of Davis Cup involvement in 1996. **Below:** Adriano Panatta's Davis Cup career as a player moved smoothly into captaincy duties in 1984.

Yannick Noah

Although he never landed a Davis Cup winner's award as a player for France, Noah certainly did the next best thing when, at the age of 31 in 1991, he took over the captaincy and lifted his colleagues to an inspiring 3–1 victory over the United States in Lyon in one of the most memorable occasions that has ever been staged, even in this venerable competition.

As a player, the final against those same United States nine years earlier in Grenoble was the closest he came, but the Americans won that one 4–1. Noah was at the heart of another classic when he duelled John McEnroe in a wonderful five-setter before being beaten 12–10 1–6 3–6 6–2 6–3.

Noah had made his Davis Cup debut in a 1978 European Zone A tie against Great Britain in Paris and, apart from absences in 1986 and 1987, was a regular in the team up to and including 1990. Noah played in 22 ties for France, amassing a 39–22 record—26 won and 15 lost in singles play, 13 won and 7 lost in doubles.

It was as captain that the sometimes wayward Noah was a revelation in 1991. He cajoled, pleaded, ranted and inspired his players to a brand of tennis they did not realise was within them. No wonder he styled himself "player-captain." Fourteen months later, he stunned all of France by abruptly resigning following his first defeat, 3–2 to Switzerland in the 1992 competition, saying, "The team doesn't need me any more." But the team did. He came back for the 1996 event and the result was another triumphant march to the final.

Left: The flair and panache which made Yannick Noah such a crowd-pleasing player are evident in this forehand volley. **Below:** Yannick Noah's transition from player to inspirational captain revived France's Davis Cup fortunes in spectacular fashion in 1991.

Stefan Edberg

Like his flawless record in the Grand Slams, Edberg possesses a marvellous record of consistency in the Davis Cup. He played on three of Sweden's Cup-winning teams, starting against the United States in 1984, following up against Germany the next year and then against Russia in 1994. Though he also played in the earlier rounds in 1987 Edberg did not compete in the final against India. He also represented his country in a losing cause in the finals of 1986 against Australia and in 1988 and 1989 against Germany.

When he announced at the start of 1996 that he intended to retire at the end of the year, Edberg thought he had played his last Davis Cup tie. He did not appear in Sweden's first round victory over Belgium or the quarter-final win in India. But so good was his autumn form, particularly at the U.S. Open, that he was brought back for the semifinal against the Czech Republic and responded with a pair of singles wins. Edberg kept his singles place for the final against France but early exit with an ankle injury meant that his career ended with a record in 35 ties of 47–23; 35 singles wins and 15 losses and 12 doubles wins against 8 losses.

Left: Stefan Edberg leaps over the net after his win in the deciding singles of the 1985 final against Germany in Munich. **Below:** Stefan Edberg's pleasant and easy-going off-court demeanour disguised steely determination when it came to Davis Cup competition.

Czechoslovakia / Czech Republic

Despite the depths of skill and talent produced by the country—first in its long years as Czechoslovakia and subsequently as the Czech Republic—the success rate in the Davis Cup has been disappointingly low. One victory in 1980 and one runner-up spot in 1975 is the sum total of their achievements.

In 1975 Jan Kodes, the man who won Wimbledon in the player boycott year of 1973, was the leading light of the Czech bid, in which they beat France in the European Zone final and then Australia in the Inter-Zone final before going down against a Bjorn Borg-inspired Sweden in Stockholm. Kodes was, over the years, the most consistent of the Czechs, appearing in 39 ties and winning 60 of his 95 matches (singles 39–20, doubles 21–15). Not far behind was Tomas Smid, who won 42 of his 67 matches in 31 ties.

The durable Smid formed the other half of the Czech squad with Ivan Lendl when Czechoslovakia won the Davis Cup for the first and, so far, only time in 1980 by beating Italy 4–1 in Prague.

Left: The young Ivan Lendl (left) and Tomas Smid celebrate doubles victory in the 1980 Davis Cup final between Czechoslovakia and Italy in Prague. **Below:** Czechoslovakia's Davis Cup-winning team of 1980: (left to right) Tomas Smid, Ivan Lendl, Pavel Slozil and Jan Kodes with team captain Antonin Bolardt and the referee, Derek Hardwick (GBR).

Final Round

Circumstances dictated that the Davis Cup by NEC Final would be staged by Sweden in their third largest city, Malmö, which has a population of 250,000. The indoor arenas of the capital, Stockholm, and the second city of Gothenburg were already booked for other events, so the choice of venue was the Malmomassan Convention Centre, which has a capacity of 4,500. As soon as tickets for the Final went on sale they were snapped up within hours.

The first snows of early winter greeted those who travelled to the Convention Centre for the draw on Thursday 28 November. In his address of welcome Jan Francke, President of the Swedish Tennis Association, recalled that the last Davis Cup tie between Sweden and France had taken place two years previously in the heat of Cannes. "So that is why we have ordered the snow to come here," he said with a smile.

Below: French captain Yannick Noah offers encouragement to his team. **Right:** Stefan Edberg

The Davis Cup itself was prominently on display on a platform at the front of the conference hall and the soberly attired teams posed with the trophy for the cameras. The French wore dark blue blazers and ties, the Swedes were in black shirts, light grey jackets and dark grey trousers. The first name to be drawn from the bowl was that of Cedric Pioline, the French number one, who would play Stefan Edberg, Sweden's number two, with Arnaud Boetsch then scheduled to face Thomas Enqvist in the second match of the opening day.

It was, said Sweden's captain, Carl-Axel Hageskog, a good draw for his team "because Stefan prefers a fixed start time." There were many media questions directed at Edberg on his last tennis occasion before retiring, but Edberg insisted he felt no pressure because he was part of a team.

Yannick Noah, France's captain, paid tribute to Edberg's role in tennis. "We all respect Stefan very much," he said. "We all agree he was a class player, always fair. He was a role model for a lot of people. If he had organised a party at his place we would have gone and enjoyed it with him. But he decided he wanted a party here, so we want to spoil his party."

Noah and his team had spared no effort in their spoilsport attempt. Before travel-

ling to Sweden the French squad spent a week in training at the Brittany resort of Quiberon, where an exact replica of the Malmö court had been assembled by the same Swedish builders. Here they also practised Noah's new-found interest in Zen and yoga. Still, Sweden were heavy favourites to capture their sixth Davis Cup.

Sweden's confidence lasted exactly 36 minutes into the first match when Edberg, moving in to the net, stumbled and turned his right ankle. Until then he had been holding his own, but only just, against Pioline. The French player broke for a 3–1 lead when Edberg perpetrated three volleying errors, but the Swede broke back immediately. It was in the next game, the sixth, that Edberg damaged the ankle.

After the permitted three minutes of treatment he opted to resume and even managed to hold serve from love–30, but he was wincing from the effort of pushing off to serve and was tentative in his movements. Understandably, Pioline did everything to capitalise on this unexpected bonus, moving his opponent from side to side, drawing him towards the net and lobbing him. Another break of Edberg's serve was inevitable and it duly came in the eighth game when Pioline struck a brilliant backhand pass deep into the corner. Pioline went on to serve out for the set at 6–3 but it had taken 58 minutes to complete.

Above: Cedric Pioline
Right: Stefan Edberg

With Sweden's team doctor and physiotherapist anxiously in attendance, Edberg underwent further treatment at the changeovers but it was clear the handicap was proving a severe one. Afterwards he said, "If it hadn't been Davis Cup I might have stopped, but there were a lot of things to play for. It was just a question of hanging in there and hoping for miracles."

Sadly, no miracle manifested itself and the match took its inevitable course. Pioline broke for a 2–1 lead in the second set, only for Edberg to level matters immediately, but, as in the first set, Pioline got another break of serve later on to go in front 5–4 and served out for a two-set lead. The gallant Edberg, by now limping heavily, was broken twice more in the third set and Pioline completed an unexpectedly

comfortable afternoon's work, 6–3 6–4 6–3 in two hours 27 minutes. Noah offered his player a muted high five, but celebrations were low key. Everyone felt sorry for Edberg.

In contrast to the French supporters, the Swedish majority in the audience had sat in silence for most of that opening match but in the second singles they got vociferously behind their man, Thomas Enqvist, as he battled to get Sweden back on level terms against Boetsch. The Frenchman, outmatched physically, was also unable to counter Enqvist's greater power of shot. The sheer ferocity of some of Enqvist's ground-strokes had the crowd gasping as he broke in the tenth game to capture the first set.

Left: Thomas Enqvist
Above: Arnaud Boetsch

Enqvist had closed out the circuit season in peak form, winning tournaments in Paris and Stockholm, and he went boldly for victory. Too boldly on occasion, since most of Boetsch's points were gathered from Enqvist errors as he pressed with excessive zeal for the big winners. After 69 minutes Enqvist served out to love to win the second set 6–3, and when he immediately broke serve in the opening game of the third set the Swede moved his attacking strategy up another notch. Aces alternated with double faults as Enqvist bore down, and he paid the price when Boetsch broke back, courtesy of four Swedish errors, to pull level at 4–4. That was enough to send the third set into a tiebreak, but for Boetsch it was merely delaying the end. Enqvist dominated the tiebreak, by seven points to two, just as he had dominated the match, 6–4 6–4 7–6. So, at the end of the day, Sweden were level at 1–1 and happy to be in that position in view of the earlier misfortunes.

With Edberg's further participation in doubt, victory in the doubles was of crucial importance for Sweden. In their nine previous appearances in the Davis Cup Final Sweden had won five times. On all five occasions they were successful in the doubles. In their four losing finals they had been beaten in the doubles. France, it later transpired, had run into a problem with their plans because Guy Forget's long-term knee injury was playing up. But the 31-year-old lefthander, playing in his 25th Davis Cup tie 12 years after his debut, declared himself fit and lined up alongside Guillaume Raoux. Forget's Davis Cup doubles involvement stretched back over 11 years and 23 matches (20 won, three lost) but in only two of those matches had he been partnered by Raoux, both of them in the 1996 Cup run. Likewise, the Swedish combination of Nicklas Kulti and Jonas Bjorkman had been fashioned during the 1996 competition and this was only their fourth match together.

Above: Guillaume Raoux (on left) and Guy Forget, the winning doubles combination. **Right:** Sweden's last-day hero, Nicklas Kulti.

Having been comprehensively outshouted on the opening day, Swedish supporters turned up in better voice, and more exotically garbed, for the second day's battle. There were Viking horns, faces painted in the national colours of blue and yellow and banners in abundance. But the French minority, with their klaxons, drums, whistles and pom poms, still managed to make more noise on a decidedly raucous occasion.

It was a strange doubles contest of wildly swinging fortunes played at a brutal pace, and it was the serving weaknesses of Bjorkman, who was broken four times, that cost Sweden the match they so desperately needed to win. The first break gave France a 3–1 first set lead, and Forget's elegant backhand return which achieved that break had Noah and the rest of the French bench on their feet exulting. Having taken the opening set 6–3, Forget and Raoux were then comprehensively outplayed in the second when, from 1–1, the Swedes won five games in succession, capturing the last 14 points.

No sooner had the Swedish players finished congratulating each other than they were on the rack again. France surged 5–0 up in the third set, conceding only five points in those five games. Sweden managed to apply the brake and there was a momentary wobble for France when the stocky, bespectacled Raoux dropped serve. But they came through it, took the second set 6–3 and then set about Bjorkman again in the fourth set. He was broken for a third time as Sweden went behind 3–2 and when he served again, at 3–5 and trying to keep his country alive, Bjorkman found himself match point down after netting a backhand volley. It was the only invitation France needed. Forget struck another stunning backhand service return down the line and victory was theirs, by a score of 6–3 1–6 6–3 6–3, in two and a quarter hours.

An hour after that match, in a now-deserted arena, there was more drama as Edberg,

his right leg taped to mid-calf, appeared for a fitness test. He jogged half a dozen circuits of the court, had a gentle hit for 20 minutes and then left with a smile but no comment. The next morning there was a further workout for Edberg, after which it was decided at a Swedish team meeting that his place in the final singles would be taken by Kulti, though no announcement was made. Afterwards Edberg said, "I felt it was not right for me to play and though it was hard, that was the right decision. If you aren't 100 percent fit in tennis today your chances of winning decrease quite a bit. I was not 100 percent and that was really the point."

So Enqvist went on court not only well aware that he needed a victory over Cedric Pioline to keep Sweden's hopes alive but that, if he proved successful, his nation's hopes would then depend on an inexperienced substitute.

For day three, Swedish support was at its noisiest level yet and the arena was awash with flags. For a change, the French fans were outshouted. Enqvist's attempts to dominate Pioline with naked power, as he had done against Boetsch, were frustrated by Pioline's topspin style. "So it was harder for me to step in and hit winners," Enqvist explained later. It was difficult, in fact, for Enqvist to do much at all. He lost the first set in 31 minutes, with Pioline conceding a mere four points in five service games. With the Swede still prone to error and uncertainty, Pioline continued to prosper as the second set moved into a

Left: Cedric Pioline
Above: Thomas Enqvist

tiebreak. Here Enqvist had a chance when he stood at set point but after a beautifully worked rally left him with a simple forehand into an open court, he hit the top of the net instead. Later, Enqvist called it "the easiest forehand of my life." It might also have proved one of the costliest. Pioline went on to take that tiebreak by ten points to eight for a two-set lead and though Enqvist, now hitting more freely, took the third and fourth sets by the score of 6–4, he was soon in trouble in the decider.

An early break of serve left Pioline leading 4–1, with every French point greeted by uproar. Then, at 5–3, the Frenchman served for the match and the Cup after three hours 45 minutes. Forty minutes later he had been beaten. Three forehand errors cost

Pioline that service game. At 5–5 Pioline saved a break point which would have left Enqvist serving for the match but in the fifth set's 15th game the break finally came—and it fell Sweden's way. Though two of Enqvist's shots were stunning forehand service returns, he also collected a couple of lucky points, the first with a mishit that fell on the line and then when Pioline double-faulted on break point.

Still the heart-stopping drama was not over. Enqvist also double-faulted to give Pioline a point to break back but then saved it with a brave forehand winner. A backhand down the line gave the Swede match point, at which a weary Pioline pro-

jected a forehand service return beyond the baseline. The 3–6 6–7 6–4 6–4 9–7 victory had taken four hours 25 minutes.

As the hoarse supporters headed for the refreshment stands, none of them could have dreamed that the real excitement on this dramatic and historic final day was only just beginning. Now the formal announcement was made that Kulti, and not Edberg, would be playing Boetsch in the deciding singles. The omens were not good for Sweden. Boetsch had won both their previous matches and, since he finished as champion at the Halle tournament in June, Kulti had won only one singles. That, ironically, had been the match in Stockholm that ended Edberg's career on the tour.

The 24-year-old Kulti was ranked 65 in the world, and the 27-year-old, fresh-faced Boetsch 33rd. But in the heat of Davis Cup battle such rankings are irrelevant. Stoicism, fortitude and stamina are the key ingredients. Kulti should have stood little chance against an experienced Davis Cup campaigner and, in his baggy shorts and Paisley bandanna, he hardly looked cast as the hero his team captain, Carl-Axel Hageskog, had said he was looking for if this final went the distance.

But Boetsch soon found himself disconcerted by Kulti's big hitting and determination. The Frenchman survived a break point as early as the fourth game and then escaped two set points when trailing 6–5. Offered the "escape clause" of a tiebreak, Boetsch seized it, winning by seven points to two to go one set up after 64 minutes' play.

With Edberg cheering on his replacement from a crowded Swedish team bench, Kulti set about demolishing Boetsch's service game. He achieved two breaks to win the

second set and had the Swedish fans in full-throated chorus as he survived a total of nine break points in the third set and, incredibly, won it to go in front by two sets to one. By now Yannick Noah was working overtime on man-management of his demoralised player. Boetsch responded well and led 4–1 in the fourth set, only to be pegged back by an opponent who simply refused to acknowledge the prospect of defeat. Kulti again took the set to a tiebreak, again perpetrated crucial errors and, just as he found himself set point down, was stricken by cramp in his right leg. As he hobbled around, attempting at one stage to halt play to obtain treatment—and, quite correctly, being refused—Kulti orchestrated a demonstration by Swedish supporters that created enough noise to give him precious seconds to recover.

Left: Nicklas Kulti
Below: Arnaud Boetsch

There was no stopping Boetsch at this stage, however. He won the tiebreak seven points to five and, after three hours 33 minutes, this pulsating deciding rubber was level again at two sets all. But now Kulti's cramp had tilted the odds in France's favour. The Swede stood up at every changeover, afraid that if he sat down he would never manage to get up again. His legs were massaged by his captain, he took aboard food and liquid and went out, to a torrent of support from the stands, to do battle against his opponent and his physical ailment.

With the advantage of serving first in that fifth set, Kulti got his nose in front and managed to keep it there. Incredibly, with the stakes so high and considering the nerve-shredding responsibility, neither man faced a break point on his own serve for 13 straight games, though at one point Boetsch's accuracy and stamina started to waver and he, too, began to get a rub-down from his captain at the changeovers.

Then suddenly, with the dramatic impact of an explosion, disaster stared France full in the face. With Kulti leading 7–6, Boetsch's next service game got off to a poor start with a double fault. Love–15. Then a Kulti forehand return clipped the baseline. Love–30. The Swedish fans bellowed their joy. Next a weak second serve was pun-

ished by a forehand winning return. Love–40. Three Cup-winning points for Sweden.

As his teammates offered anxious support, Boetsch calmly set about restoring their hopes. By now, after four hours 28 minutes' play, Kulti was seriously hobbled by his cramp and, incredibly, all three match points got away from him. First he sent a backhand wide, then Boetsch pulled out a fine service winner and finally a backhand return sailed high and wide. With the help of an authoritative smash and another Kulti backhand error France were off the hook. In the packed stands Swedes were silent, French exulted.

Three games later it was Kulti's turn on the rack. As he fell love–40 behind on serve, the Swede pulled up with a grimace, his right leg twitching. He lost the next point too, netting a backhand, before hobbling to the sidelines for sustenance and assistance, leaving Boetsch to contemplate serving for the match, the Davis Cup, and glory. He had already just won six points in a row to set up victory. Now he rapidly made it nine, thanks to an ace and a couple of Kulti errors. Forty–love; three points for the Cup. Bravely, incredibly, Kulti saved two of them but on the third he struck a forehand fractionally over the baseline. After four hours 47 minutes, Boetsch had finally put away his unfancied opponent 7–6 2–6 4–6 7–6 10–8 and France were Davis Cup champions.

Boetsch's teammates poured over the low courtside advertising hoarding and bore him aloft in triumph. And then, more than an hour later, after the ceremonies, congratulations and celebrations, the French team arrived for their media conference, preceded by a waiter bearing a tray of beer. As he sipped from a plastic glass Noah was eventually asked what he thought about France's chances in the opening round of the 1997 Davis Cup against Australia, only two months away. With a grimace, the French captain said he didn't even want to think about that right now, never mind talk about it. "This is the time for some champagne and some beer," he said with a smile.

Left: Arnaud Boetsch is somewhere between disbelief and jubilation as France gain the Cup-winning point. **Above:** Yannick Noah and Guy Forget celebrate France's victory.

● **DAVIS CUP BY NEC 1996 WORLD GROUP** Seeding: Russia, USA, Germany, Sweden, France, Netherlands, Austria and Czech Republic.
● **FIRST ROUND** (9-11 February) - Italy d. Russia 3-2, Rome ITA: A. Gaudenzi (ITA) d. A. Chesnokov (RUS) 2–6 6–7(5) 7–6(5) 6–3 6–1; Y. Kafelnikov (RUS) d. R. Furlan (ITA) 6–3 7–5 6–4 6–3; A. Gaudenzi/D. Nargiso (ITA) d. Y. Kafelnikov/A. Olhovskiy (RUS) 6–4 2–6 7–5 7–6(4) 6–4; Y. Kafelnikov (RUS) d. A. Gaudenzi (ITA) 6–3 3–6 7–6(4) 7–5; R. Furlan (ITA) d. A. Chesnokov (RUS) 6–0 3–6 6–3 7–5. South Africa d. Austria 3-2, Johannesburg RSA: T. Muster (AUT) d. M. Ondruska (RSA) 6–2 7–5 6–2; W. Ferreira (RSA) d. W. Schranz (AUT) 6 1 7–6(2) 6–4; W. Ferreira/G. Muller (RSA) d. A. Antonitsch/T. Muster 6–3 7–6(3) 6–7(5) 3–6 6–3; T. Muster (AUT) d. W. Ferreira (RSA) 7–5 6–7(5) 6–4 7–6(4); M. Ondruska (RSA) d. G. Schaller (AUT) 6–3 6–4 6–2. Germany d. Switzerland 5-0, Geneva SUI: D. Prinosil (GER) d. J. Hlasek (SUI) 6–4 7–6(4) 7–5 4–6 6–1; H. Dreekmann (GER) d. M. Rosset (SUI) 6–3 6–1 6–4; D. Prinosil/M. Stich (GER) d. J. Hlasek/A. Strambini (SUI) 6–2 7–5 6–2; D. Prinosil (GER) d. A. Strambini (SUI) 6–3 6–3; H. Dreekmann (GER) d. J. Hlasek (SUI) 6–4 6–4. France d. Denmark 5-0, Besancon FRA: G. Forget (FRA) d. K. Carlsen (DEN) 6–4 7–6(3) 7–5 7–6(7); C. Pioline (FRA) d. F. Fetterlein (DEN) 4–6 6–1 6–1 6–3; G. Forget/G. Raoux (FRA) d. K. Carlsen/F. Fetterlein (DEN) 4–6 6–3 7–6(4) 6–3; C. Pioline (FRA) d. K. Carlsen (DEN) 7–5 6–4; G. Raoux (FRA) d. F. Fetterlein (DEN) 6–3 6–4. India d. Netherlands 3-2, Jaipur IND: J. Eltingh (NED) d. L. Paes (IND) 6–4 7–5 6–4; M. Bhupathi (IND) d. J. Siemerink (NED) 6–4 7–6(4) 4–6 4–6 6–4; J. Eltingh/P. Haarhuis (NED) d. L. Paes/M. Bhupathi (IND) 3–6 6–2 7–6(3) 6–4; L. Paes (IND) d. J. Siemerink (NED) 7–6(2) 2–6 7–6(3) 7–6(5); M. Bhupathi (IND) d. J. Eltingh (NED) 7–6(4) 4–6 7–5 2-1. Sweden d. Belgium 4-1, Katrineholm SWE: M. Larsson (SWE) d. F. de Wulf (BEL) 6–3 7–5 7–6(4); T. Enqvist (SWE) d. D. Norman (BEL) 6–4 6–3 6–1; J. Bjorkman/N. Kulti (SWE) d. F. de Wulf/D. Norman (BEL) 6–3 6–1 6–4; J. van Herck (BEL) d. T. Enqvist (SWE) 7–5 6–2; M. Larsson (SWE) d. D. Norman (BEL) 7–6(3) 6–4. Czech Republic d. Hungary 5-0, Plzen CZE: D. Vacek (CZE) v. J. Krocsko (HUN) 6–3 6–3 6–4; P. Korda (CZE) d. S. Noszaly (HUN) 6–2 7–6(4) 6–3; C. Suk/D. Vacek (CZE) d. G. Koves/S. Noszaly (HUN) 6–7(2) 6–7(7) 7–6(7) 6–4 6–4; D. Vacek (CZE) d. S. Noszaly (HUN) 7–5 6–3; J. Novak (CZE) d. J. Krocsko (HUN) 7–5 7–6(4) 6–0. USA d. Mexico 5-0, Carlsbad USA: M. Chang (USA) d. L. Lavalle (MEX) 6–1 6–2 6–4; T. Martin (USA) d. A. Hernandez (MEX) 6–3 6–3 6–0; P. Galbraith/P. McEnroe (USA) d. L. Lavalle/O. Ortiz (MEX) 7–6(7) 6–4 6–3; M. Chang (USA) d. A. Hernandez (MEX) 6–0 6–2; T. Martin (USA) d. L. Lavalle (MEX) 3–6 7–6(1) 6–4. ● **QUARTERFINALS** (7–5 April) - Italy d. South Africa 4-1, Rome ITA: M. Ondruska (RSA) d. R. Furlan (ITA) 6–4 6–4 6–4; A. Gaudenzi (ITA) d. W. Ferreira (RSA) 7–5 6–3 2–6 7–5 6–1; A. Gaudenzi/D. Nargiso (ITA) d. E. Ferreira/W. Ferreira (RSA) 7–5 3–6 6–3 7–6(7) 6–2; R. Furlan (ITA) d. W. Ferreira (RSA) 3–6 6–0 7–6(4) 6–2; A. Gaudenzi (ITA) d. M. Ondruska (RSA) 6–1 1-1 ret. France d. Germany 5-0, Limoges FRA: C. Pioline (FRA) d. D. Prinosil (GER) 6–0 6–7(6) 6–4 6–3; A. Boetsch (FRA) d. H. Dreekmann (GER) 4–6 6–4 3–6 7–6(2) 6–3; A. Boetsch/G. Forget (FRA) d. B. Becker/M-K. Goellner (GER) 7–6(6) 6–4 7–6(7); G. Forget (FRA) d. D. Prinosil (GER) 6–3 0–6 6–4; C. Pioline (FRA) d. H. Dreekmann (GER) 6–4 6–3. Sweden d. India 5-0, Calcutta IND: J. Bjorkman (SWE) d. L. Paes (IND) 1–6 6–4 7–5 6–3 7–5; T. Enqvist (SWE) d. M. Bhupathi (IND) 6–7(5) 7–6(3) 6–1 6–1; J. Bjorkman/N. Kulti (SWE) d. M. Bhupathi/L. Paes (IND) 6–7(4) 6–3 6–4 6–1; N. Kulti (SWE) d. L. Paes (IND) 6–3 6–7(4) 7–6(6); J. Bjorkman (SWE) d. M. Bhupathi (IND) 6–2 6–4. Czech Republic d. USA 3-2, Prague CZE: T. Martin (USA) d. P. Korda (CZE) 6–2 6–4 7–5; D. Vacek (CZE) d. M. Washington (USA) 4–6 6–3 6–4 7–5 6–4; P. Korda/D. Vacek (CZE) d. P. Galbraith/P. McEnroe (USA) 6–2 6–3 6–3; T. Martin (USA) d. D. Vacek (CZE) 7–6(1) 6–3 6–1; P. Korda (CZE) d. M. Washington (USA) 7–6(5) 6–3 6–2. ● **SEMI-FINALS** (20-22 September) - France d. Italy 3-2, Nantes FRA: A. Gaudenzi (ITA) d. C. Pioline (FRA) 5–7 6–1 7–6(4) 6–3; R. Furlan (ITA) d. A. Boetsch (FRA) 7–5 1–6 6–3 7–6(5); G. Forget/G. Raoux (FRA) d. A. Gaudenzi/D. Nargiso (ITA) 6–3 6–4 6–2; C. Pioline (FRA) d. R. Furlan (ITA) 6–3 2–6 6–2 6–4; A. Boetsch (FRA) d. A. Gaudenzi (ITA) 6–4 6–2 7–6(8). Sweden d. Czech Republic 4-1, Prague CZE: T. Enqvist (SWE) d. P. Korda (CZE) 6–4 6–3 7–6(9); S. Edberg (SWE) d. D. Vacek (CZE) 7–6(2) 7–5 4–6 6–3; P. Korda/D. Vacek (CZE) d. J. Bjorkman/N. Kulti (SWE) 4–6 6–3 6–4 6–4; T. Enqvist (SWE) d. D. Vacek (CZE) 6–3 6–7(3) 4–6 7–5 6–3; S. Edberg (SWE) d. P. Korda (CZE) 4–6 6–2 7–5. ● **FINAL (29 NOVEMBER - 1 DECEMBER)** - France d. Sweden 3–2, Malmo SWE: C. Pioline (FRA) d. S. Edberg (SWE) 6–3 6–4 6–3; T. Enqvist (SWE) d. A. Boetsch (FRA) 6–4 6–3 7–6(2); G. Forget/G. Raoux (FRA) d. J. Bjorkman/N. Kulti (SWE) 6–3 1–6 6–3 6–3; T. Enqvist (SWE) d. C. Pioline (FRA) 3–6 6–7(8) 6–4 6–4 9–7; A. Boetsch (FRA) d. N. Kulti (SWE) 7–6(2) 2–6 4–6 7–7(5) 10–8.

● **QUALIFYING ROUND FOR WORLD GROUP (20-22 SEPTEMBER)** - Mexico d. Argentina 3-2, Mexico City MEX: A. Hernandez (MEX) d. G. Etlis (ARG) 7–6(5) 6–2 6–4; H. Gumy (ARG) d. L. Lavalle (MEX) 7–6(5) 6–4 4–6 5–7 7–5; A. Hernandez/O. Ortiz (MEX) d. P. Albano/L. Lobo (ARG) 6–7(5) 6–4 3–6 7–6(2) 6–4; A. Hernandez (MEX) d. H. Gumy (ARG) 6–4 7–5 6–1; G. Etlis (ARG) d. L. Lavalle (MEX) 6–3 3–6 ret. Australia d. Croatia 4-1, Split CRO: M. Philippoussis (AUS) d. S. Hirszon (CRO) 6–2 6–3 6–2; J. Stoltenberg (AUS) d. G. Ivanisevic (CRO) 4–6 6–3 3–6 7–6(5) 6–2; P. Rafter/M. Woodforde (AUS) d. S. Hirszon/G. Ivanisevic (CRO) 6–3 6–2 6–4; M. Philippoussis (AUS) d. G. Oresic (CRO) 6–1 6–4; S. Hirszon (CRO) d. J. Stoltenberg (AUS) 6–2 6–2. Brazil d. Austria 4-1, São Paulo BRA: T. Muster (AUT) d. F. Meligeni (BRA) 6–3 6–3 6–3; G. Kuerten (BRA) d. M. Hipfl (AUT) 4–6 3–6 7–6(0) 7–6(5) 6–1; G. Kuerten/J. Oncins (BRA) d. T. Muster/U. Plamberger (AUT) 7–6(2) 4–6 6–3 3–6 2–0 (defaulted). Austria defaulted the two remaining singles. Romania d. Belgium 3-2, Bucharest ROM: J. van Herck (BEL) d. A. Voinea (ROM) 6–7(6) 6–4 6–2 6–1; A. Pavel (ROM) d. F. Dewulf (BEL) 6–1 6–3 6–2; F. Dewulf/P. Pimek (BEL) d. G. Cosac/D. Pescariu (ROM) 4–6 6–0 6–2 6–4; A. Voinea (ROM) d. F. Dewulf (BEL) 6–0 6–0 6–2; A. Pavel (ROM) d. J. van Herck (BEL) 6–3 6–4 6–3. Netherlands d. New Zealand 4-1, Haarlem NED: J. Siemerink (NED) d. B. Steven (NZL) 6–7(4) 7–6(2) 6–3 3–6 6–2; A. Hunt (NZL) d. R. Krajicek (NED) 7–6(5) 3–6 4–6 4–1 ret; J. Siemerink/S. Schalken (NED) d. A. Hunt/B. Steven (NZL) 3–6 7–6(6) 6–4 6–2; S. Schalken (NED) d. J. Greenhalgh (NZL) 7–5 6–1 6–7(5) 6–1; D. van Scheppingen (NED) d. A. Hunt (NZL) 6–3 7–6(6). Russia d. Hungary 4-1, Moscow RUS: Y. Kafelnikov (RUS) d. A. Savolt (HUN) 7–5 3–6 6–3 6–4; A. Chesnokov (RUS) d. J. Krocsko (HUN) 6–2 6–2 6–2; Y. Kafelnikov/A. Olhovskiy (RUS) d. G. Koves/S. Noszaly (HUN) 7–6(2) 6–3 6–1; Y. Kafelnikov (RUS) d. J. Krocsko (HUN) 6–0 6–3; A. Savolt (HUN) d. A. Chesnokov (RUS) 6–3 6–2. Spain d. Denmark 4-1, Tarragona ESP: A. Costa (ESP) d. F. Fetterlein (DEN) 6–0 6–0 6–2; C. Moya (ESP) d. K. Carlsen (DEN) 6–1 6–2 6–1; T. Carbonell/A. Corretja (ESP) d. K. Carlsen/F. Fetterlein (DEN) 6–4 7–5 4–6 5–7 6–3; K. Carlsen (DEN) d. A. Costa (ESP) 3–6 7–5 6–3; C. Moya (ESP) d. T. Larsen (DEN) 6–3 6–4. Switzerland d. Morocco 5-0, Olten SUI: J. Hlasek (SUI) d. M. Tahiri (MAR) 0–6 6–3 6–2 7–5; M. Rosset (SUI) d. M. El Aarej (MAR) 6–0 6–1 6–3; J. Hlasek/M. Rosset (SUI) d. M. El Aarej/M. Tahiri (MAR) 6–2 6–2 6–0; M. Rosset (SUI) d. M. Tahiri (MAR) 3–6 6–3 6–1; J. Hlasek (SUI) d. L. Rharnit (MAR) 6–0 6–1. The winners of these eight ties qualified for the World Group for the 1997 competition. The losers remained in, or were relegated to, their respective Group 1 Zones for the 1996 competition.
● **GROUP I EURO/AFRICAN ZONE** Seeding: Morocco, Spain, Romania and Croatia. ● **FIRST ROUND** (9-11 February) - Israel d. Norway 3-2,

Tel Aviv ISR: C. Ruud (NOR) d. N. Behr (ISR) 7–6(5) 6–2 6–2; E. Ran (ISR) d. H. Koll (NOR) 6–1 6–2 6–4; E. Erlich/E. Ran (ISR) d. H. Koll/C. Ruud (NOR) 3–6 6–7(5) 7–5 6–3 6–4; C. Ruud (NOR) d. E. Ran (ISR) 7–5 6–7(5) 6–7(4) 6–3 6–1; E. Erlich (ISR) d. H. Koll (NOR) 6–4 1–6 6–4 7–6(4). ● **SECOND ROUND** (7–5 April) - Spain d. Israel 4-1, Tel Aviv ISR: C. Costa (ESP) d. E. Ran (ISR) 3–6 6–3 6–4 2-0 ret; A. Costa (ESP) d. E. Erlich (ISR) 6–2 3–6 6–2 6–2; N. Behr/E. Erlich (ISR) d. A. Corretja/E. Sanchez (ESP) 7–5 4–6 4–6 7–6(1) 6–3; A. Costa (ESP) d. N. Behr (ISR) 6–4 6–4 6–2; C. Costa (ESP) d. E. Erlich (ISR) 7–6(1) 6–1. Croatia d. Ukraine 5-0, Dubrovnik CRO: G. Ivanisevic (CRO) d. A. Rybalko (UKR) 6–0 7–6(5) 6–7(4) 6–3; S. Hirszon (CRO) d. D. Poliakov (UKR) 6–2 6–0 6–3; S. Hirszon/G. Ivanisevic (CRO) d. D. Poliakov/A. Rybalko (UKR) 7–6(2) 6–3 6–2; I. Saric (CRO) d. V. Trotzko (UKR) 6–3 6–4; G. Oresic (CRO) d. S. Yaroshenko (UKR) 6–1 7–6(10). Romania d. Finland 3-2, Helsinki FIN: A. Pavel (ROM) d. T. Ketola (FIN) 6–4 6–2 6–4; A. Voinea (ROM) d. K. Tiilikainen (FIN) 6–1 6–2 6–4; G. Cosac/D. Pescariu (ROM) d. T. Ketola/V. Liukko (FIN) 6–2 6–4 7–6(3); T. Ketola (FIN) d. G. Cosac (ROM) 6–3 7–6(1); V. Liukko (FIN) d. A. Pavel (ROM) 6–3 6–3. Morocco d. Zimbabwe 4-1, Casablanca MAR: W. Black (ZIM) d. K. Alami (MAR) 7–5 3–6 7–5 1–6 6–2; H. Arazi (MAR) d. B. Black (ZIM) 6–3 6–2 6–1; K. Alami/H. Arazi (MAR) d. B. Black/W. Black (ZIM) 6–1 3–6 7–6(5) 6–7(4) 6–3; K. Alami (MAR) d. M. Birch (ZIM) 6–3 6–0 6–1; H. Arazi (MAR) d. W. Black (ZIM) 6–3 7–6(5). Morocco, Romania, Croatia and Spain qualified for the World Group Qualifying Round. ● **RELEGATION ROUND** (20-22 SEPTEMBER) - Zimbabwe d. Finland 4-1, Harare ZIM: W. Black (ZIM) d. K. Tiilikainen (FIN) 6–4 7–5 6–7(3) 6–3; B. Black (ZIM) d. V. Liukko (FIN) 6–3 6–3 6–4; B. Black/W. Black (ZIM) d. V. Liukko/K. Tiilikainen (FIN) 6–1 6–1 6–3; B. Black (ZIM) d. T. Nurminen (FIN) 6–7(7) 6–4 6–3; V. Liukko (FIN) d. G. Chidzikwe (ZIM) 6–1 7–6(1). Ukraine d. Norway 4-1, Kiev UKR: A. Medvedev (UKR) d. J. Frode Andersen (NOR) 6–2 6–2 6–0; A. Rybalko (UKR) d. C. Ruud (NOR) 7–6(7) 6–4 6–4; A. Medvedev/D. Poliakov (UKR) d. C. Ruud/H. Koll (NOR) 6–0 6–0 6–1; A. Medvedev (UKR) d. C. Ruud (NOR) 3–6 6–4 6–3; J. Frode Andersen (NOR) d. D. Yakimenko (UKR) 7–6(2) 6–4 .Finland and Norway were relegated to Euro/African Group II for the 1997 competition.

● **AMERICAN ZONE** Seeding: Argentina and Venezuela. ● **FIRST ROUND** (9-11 February) - Bahamas d. Peru 3-2, Nassau BAH: J. Yzaga (PER) d. R. Smith (BAH) 4–6 6–3 6–7(5) 7–5 6–1; M. Knowles (BAH) d. A. Venero (PER) 6–4 6–3 6–1; M. Knowles/R. Smith (BAH) d. J L. Noriega/J. Yzaga (PER) 6–3 6–3 7–6(6); M. Knowles (BAH) d. J. Yzaga (PER) 2–6 7–5 7–6(2) 6–3; A. Venero (PER) d. R. Smith (BAH) 6–4 6–4. Brazil d. Chile 3-2, Santiago CHI: F. Meligeni (BRA) d. S. Cortes (CHI) 6–1 6–1 7–5; M. Rios (CHI) d. J. Oncins (BRA) 6–3 6–2 7–5; G. Kuerten/J. Oncins (BRA) d. M. Rebolledo/M. Rios (CHI) 7–5 6–3 4–6 6–2; M. Rios (CHI) d. F. Meligeni (BRA) 6–2 7–6(2) 6–3; J. Oncins (BRA) d. S. Cortes (CHI) 6–3 6–4 7–5. Venezuela d. Canada 3-2, Valencia VEN: N. Pereira (VEN) d. D. Nestor (CAN) 6–4 3–6 6–3 2–6 6–4; J. Szymanski (VEN) d. S. Lareau (CAN) 7–6(4) 0–6 6–2 6–4; G. Connell/S. Lareau (CAN) d. J C. Bianchi/N. Pereira (VEN) 6–4 6–4 7–6(4); S. Lareau (CAN) d. N. Pereira (VEN) 6–7(5) 6–3 6–3 6–3; J. Szymanski (VEN) d. A. Chang (CAN) 6–3 7–5 6–3 6–2. ● **SECOND ROUND** (7–5 April) - Brazil d. Venezuela 4-1, Santos BRA: G. Kuerten (BRA) d. N. Pereira (VEN) 6–2 6–7(2) 6–1 6–2; F. Meligeni (BRA) d. J. Szymanski (VEN) 6–3 7–6(2) 6–4; N. Pereira/J. Szymanski (VEN) d. J. Oncins/F. Roese (BRA) 3–6 6–2 6–4 3–6 6–3; F. Meligeni (BRA) d. N. Pereira (VEN) 6–4 6–4 6–3; G. Kuerten (BRA) d. J. Szymanski (VEN) 6–2 6–7(6) 6–0. Argentina d. Bahamas 4-1, Mar del Plata ARG: J. Frana (ARG) d. R. Smith (BAH) 6–3 6–3 6–4; H. Gumy (ARG) d. M. Knowles (BAH) 6–3 7–6(3) 6–1; J. Frana/L. Lobo (ARG) d. M. Knowles/R. Smith (BAH) 6–4 3–6 6–2 6–3; M. Knowles (BAH) d. J. Frana (ARG) 6–7(7) 6–2 6–3; H. Gumy (ARG) d. R. Smith (BAH) 6–1 6–1. Argentina and Brazil qualified for the World Group Qualifying Round. ● **RELEGATION FIRST ROUND** (7–5 April) - Canada d. Chile 3-2, Edmonton CAN: M. Rios (CHI) d. D. Nestor (CAN) 6–4 7–6(6) 6–7(5) 3–6 14–12; S. Lareau (CAN) d. O. Bustos (CHI) 6–4 6–2 6–3; G. Connell/S. Lareau (CAN) d. O. Bustos/M. Rios (CHI) 6–3 6–4 7–5; S. Lareau (CAN) d. N. Massu (CHI) 6–3 6–1 6–3; O. Bustos (CHI) d. A. Sznajder (CAN) 6–3 6–3. ● **RELEGATION FINAL** (20-22 SEPTEMBER) - Chile d. Peru 5-0, Santiago CHI: M. Rios (CHI) d. A. Venero (PER) 7–5 6–2 6–4; G. Silberstein (CHI) d. A. Aramburu (PER) 6–0 6–4 6–3; O. Bustos/M. Rios (CHI) d. L. Horna/A. Venero (PER) 6–4 6–3 6–7(4) 3–6 8–6; M. Rios (CHI) d. A. Aramburu (PER) 6–2 6–3; G. Silberstein (CHI) d. A. Venero (PER) 7–5 6–7(7) 6–1. Peru were relegated to American Group II for the 1997 competition.

● **ASIA/OCEANIA ZONE** Seeding: New Zealand, Australia, Korea and Japan. ● **FIRST ROUND** (9-11 February) - New Zealand d. China 4-1, Christchurch NZL: B. Steven (NZL) d. Y. Zheng (CHN) 6–0 6–1 6–2; J-P. Xia (CHN) d. A. Hunt (NZL) 6–3 3–6 6–4 7–5; J. Greenhalgh/B. Steven (NZL) d. J-P. Xia/X. Xu (CHN) 6–0 6–1 6–1; B. Steven (NZL) d. J-P. Xia (CHN) 6–4 6–2 6–1; A. Hunt (NZL) d. Y. Zheng (CHN) 6–1 6–4. Korea d. Indonesia 4-1, Jakarta INA: Y-I. Yoon (KOR) d. S. Suwandi (INA) 6–4 6–0 6–2; H-T. Lee (KOR) d. A. Raturandang (INA) 6–2 4–6 6–2 6–2; S. Suwandi/E. Kusdaryanto (INA) d. E-J. Chang/H-T. Lee (KOR) 4–6 6–7(3) 7–6(8) 6–3 6–2; H-T. Lee (KOR) d. S. Suwandi (INA) 3–6 6–2 6–4 6–3; Y-I. Yoon (KOR) d. A. Raturandang (INA) 7–6(3) 4–6 7–6(5); Japan d. Philippines 5-0, Yokkaichi City JPN: S. Matsuoka (JPN) d. S. Palahang (PHI) 6–1 6–0 6–2; H. Kaneko (JPN) d. J. Lizardo (PHI) 6–4 6–0 6–1; S. Iwabuchi/T. Suzuki (JPN) d. R. Angelo/S. Palahang (PHI) 6–2 6–3 6–2; T. Suzuki (JPN) d. J. Lizardo (PHI) 6–0 6–3; H. Kaneko (JPN) d. S. Palahang (PHI) 6–2 6–1. Australia d. Chinese Taipei 3-0, Melbourne AUS: J. Stoltenberg (AUS) d. C-J. Chen (TPE) 6–1 6–2 7–6(1); T. Woodbridge (AUS) d. W-J. Chen (TPE) 6–2 6–1 6–2; R. Fromberg/T. Woodbridge (AUS) d. C-J. Chen/Y-H. Lien (TPE) 6–4 6–4 6–2; T. Woodbridge (AUS) vs C-J. Chen (TPE); J. Stoltenberg (AUS) vs W-J. Chen (TPE). Reverse singles (dead rubbers) not played due to delay of commencement of tie and result of tie known after first three rubbers. ● **SECOND ROUND** (7–5 April) - New Zealand d. Korea 3-2, Seoul KOR: H-T. Lee (KOR) d. S. Downs (NZL) 7–5 6–1 6–1; B. Steven (NZL) d. Y-I. Yoon (KOR) 6–3 1–6 6–2 6–2; A. Hunt/B. Steven (NZL) d. H-T. Lee/J-M. Lee (KOR) 4–6 6–1 6–2 7–6(4); Y-I. Yoon (KOR) d. S. Downs (NZL) 2–6 6–2 6–4 7–5; B. Steven (NZL) d. H-T. Lee (KOR) 6–4 3–6 6–3 7–6(7). Australia d. Japan 5-0, Ozaka JPN: T. Woodbridge (AUS) d. H. Kaneko (JPN) 4–6 6–7(4) 7–5 6–2 6–2; J. Stoltenberg (AUS) d. S. Matsuoka (JPN) 6–4 3–6 6–3 3–6 5–4 ret; T. Woodbridge/M. Woodforde (AUS) d. S. Iwabuchi/T. Suzuki (JPN) 6–3 6–1 6–3; T. Woodbridge (AUS) d. S. Matsuoka (JPN) 6–3 6–2; J. Stoltenberg (AUS) d. H. Kaneko (JPN) 6–1 6–2. New Zealand and Australia qualified for the World Group Qualifying Round. ● **RELEGATION FIRST ROUND** (7–5 April) - China d. Indonesia 5-0, Jakarta INA: B. Pan (CHN) d. A. Raturandang (INA) 6–0 6–1 7–5; J-P. Xia (CHN) d. S. Suwandi (INA) 3–6 2–6 6–1 6–1 6–1; B. Pan/J-P. Xia (CHN) d. D. Susetyo/S. DaCosta (INA) 3–6 6–4 4–6 6–3 6–4; B. Pan (CHN) d. S. Suwandi (INA) 6–3 7–6(5); J-P. Xia (CHN) d. A. Raturandang (INA) 6–3 6–4. Philippines d. Chinese Taipei 3-2, Taiwan TPE: J. Lizardo (PHI) d. C-Y. Tsai (TPE) 2–6 6–2 7–5 2-0 ret; S. Palahang (PHI) d. C-J. Chen (TPE) 1–6 4–6 6–2 6–0 6–0; C-J. Chen/Y-H. Lien (TPE) d. R. Angelo/A. Toledo (PHI) 7–5 6–1 7–5 1–6 6–3; J. Lizardo (PHI) d. C-J. Chen (TPE) 3–6 3–6 7–5 6–3 6–3; W-J. Chen (TPE) d. S. Palahang (PHI) 7–5 6–4. ● **RELEGATION FINAL** (20-22 SEPTEMBER) - Indonesia d. Chinese Taipei 3-2, Taipei TPE: C. Tsai (TPE) d. B. Wiryawan (INA) 7–5 6–4 6–3; C-J. Chen (TPE) d. A. Raturandang (INA) 6–4 6–0 6–3; S. Wibowo/B. Wiryawan (INA) d. C-J. Chen/Y-H. Lien (TPE) 6–2 6–4 6–2; A. Raturandang (INA) d. C. Tsai (TPE) 4–6 7–5 7–6(6) 6–3; B. Wiryawan (INA) d. C-J. Chen (TPE) 6–2 1–6 2–6 7–5 8–6. Chinese Taipei were relegated to Asia/Oceania Group II for the 1997 competition.

● **GROUP II EURO/AFRICAN ZONE** Seeding: Slovenia, Portugal, Egypt and Luxembourg. ● **FIRST ROUND** (3-5 May) - Great Britain d. Slovenia 4-1, Newcastle upon Tyne GBR: G. Rusedski (GBR) d. B. Urh (SLO) 6–1 6–4 6–7(0) 6–3; I. Bozic (SLO) d. M. Petchey (GBR) 6–4 6–4 4–6 6–2; N. Broad/G. Rusedski (GBR) d. G. Krusic/B. Urh (SLO) 7–6(6) 6–2 6–3; G. Rusedski (GBR) d. I. Bozic (SLO) 6–1 6–2 6–2; N. Gould

(GBR) d. B. Urh (SLO) 6–4 2–6 6–4. Ghana d. Malta 5-0, Accra GHA: F. Ofori (GHA) d. D. Delicata (MLT) 6–0 6–4 7–6(2); I. Donkor (GHA) d. M. Schembri (MLT) 6–4 6–3 6–7(5) 6–1; F. Ofori/I. Donkor (GHA) d. D. Delicata/M. Schembri (MLT) 6–1 7–6(5) 6–4; F. Ofori (GHA) d. M. Schembri (MLT) 6–4 6–4; T. Quaye (GHA) d. D. Delicata (MLT) 6–4 4–6 7–6(1). Egypt d. FYR of Macedonia 5-0, Cairo EGY: A. Ghoneim (EGY) d. O. Mikolovski (MKD) 6–0 6–2 6–3; T. El Sawy (EGY) d. L. Magdincev (MKD) 6–2 6–3 6–0; T. El Sawy/H. Hemeda (EGY) d. D. Jovanovski/O. Mikolovski (MKD) 6–1 6–4 6–2; H. Hemeda (EGY) d. O. Mikolovski (MKD) 4–6 6–1 6–0; A. Ghoneim (EGY) d. L. Magdincev (MKD) 6–2 6–1. Cote d'Ivoire d. Latvia 3-2, Jurmala LAT: Claude N'Goran (CIV) d. A. Strombachs (LAT) 6–3 6–1 6–3; G. Dzelde (LAT) d. Clement N'Goran (CIV) 7–5 6–4 6–1; Claude N'Goran/Clement N'Goran (CIV) d. G. Dzelde/A. Filimonovs (LAT) 7–6(5) 7–5 6–3; Claude N'Goran (CIV) d. G. Dzelde (LAT) 6 7(1) 6 3 6 1 6 2; A. Filimonovs (LAT) d. Clement N'Goran (CIV) 7 6(1) 6 3. Poland d. Nigeria 4 1, Warsaw POL. B. Dabrowski (POL) d. G. Adelekan (NGR) 6–1 6–1 6–3; S. Ladipo (NGR) d. A. Skrzypczak (POL) 6 3 6 4 6 3; M. Chmela/B. Dabrowski (POL) d. S. Ladipo/G. Omuta (NGR) 6–4 7–6(1) 6–2; B. Dabrowski (POL) d. S. Ladipo (NGR) 6–1 2–6 7–6(5) 6–1; A. Skrzypczak (POL) d. G. Adelekan (NGR) 6–0 6–4. Belarus d. Luxembourg 4-1, Luxembourg LUX: A. Shvec (BLR) d. P. Schaul (LUX) 6–2 7–6(1) 6–1; S. Thoma (LUX) d. V. Voltchkov (BLR) 1–6 7–5 7–6(7) 7–6(4); M. Mirnyi/V. Voltchkov (BLR) d. J. Goudenbour/A. Paris (LUX) 7–6(5) 6–2 6–7(1) 7–6(2); A. Shvec (BLR) d. S. Thoma (LUX) 7–5 6–2 3–6 2–6 6–3; V. Voltchkov (BLR) d. P. Schaul (LUX) 6–3 6–1. Slovak Republic d. Yugoslavia 4-1, Budva YUG: K. Kucera (SVK) d. N. Djordjevic (YUG) 6–1 6–3 7–5; J. Kroslak (SVK) d. B. Vujic (YUG) 4–6 6–0 6–2 6–3; D. Vemic/N. Zimonjic (YUG) d. J. Kroslak/K. Kucera (SVK) 7–5 6–4 2–6 2–6 6–3; K. Kucera (SVK) d. B. Vujic (YUG) 7–5 6–1 6–4; J. Kroslak (SVK) d. N. Djordjevic (YUG) 6–2 2–6 6–4. Portugal d. Algeria 5-0, Algiers ALG: E. Couto (POR) d. O. Hared (ALG) 6–3 6–0 6–1; B. Mota (POR) d. A-H. Hameurlaine (ALG) 6–2 6–1 6–1; E. Couto/B. Mota (POR) d. A-H. Hameurlaine/N. Hakimi (ALG) 6–3 6–1 6–0; B. Fragoso (POR) d. M. Mahmoudi (ALG) 6–4 6–4; B. Mota (POR) d. O. Hared (ALG) 6–1 6–0. ● **SECOND ROUND** (12-14 JULY) - Great Britain d. Ghana 5-0, Accra GHA: T. Henman (GBR) d. I. Donkor (GHA) 6–2 6-0 6–2; L. Milligan (GBR) d. F. Ofori (GHA) 6–1 3–6 6–4 6–2; N. Broad/M. Petchey (GBR) d. I. Donkor/F. Ofori (GHA) 6–1 6–4 6–1; T. Henman (GBR) d. D. Omaboe (GHA) 6–3 4–6 6-0; L. Milligan (GBR) d. I. Donkor (GHA) 6–4 6–3. Egypt d. Cote D'Ivoire 3-2, Cairo EGY: T. El Sawy (EGY) d. Clement N'Goran (CIV) 6–2 7–5 6–2; A. Ghoneim (EGY) d. Claude N'Goran (CIV) 3–6 6–3 6–1 4–6 6–3; Clement N'Goran/Claude N'Goran (CIV) d. T. El Sawy/H. Hemeida (EGY) 6–1 6–1 6–3; T. El Sawy (EGY) d. Claude N'Goran (CIV) 6–4 6–2 6–1; Clement N'Goran (CIV) d. A. Ghoneim (EGY) 6–3 6–4. Poland d. Belarus 4-1, Poznan POL: B. Dabrowski (POL) d. A. Shvec (BLR) 7–5 6–2 6–4; A. Skrzypczak (POL) d. M. Mirnyi (BLR) 6–3 6–2 6–3; M. Mirnyi/V. Voltchkov (BLR) d. M. Chmela/B. Dabrowski (POL) 6–4 4–6 6–3 6–2; B. Dabrowski (POL) d. M. Mirnyi (BLR) 6–4 7–5 6–1; A. Skrzypczak (POL) d. V. Voltchkov (BLR) 7–6(1) 6–3. Slovak Republic d. Portugal 5-0, Trnava SVK: J. Kroslak (SVK) d. E. Couto (POR) 6-0 6–4 6–1; K. Kucera (SVK) d. N. Marques (POR) 7–6(2) 2–6 6–4 6–4; J. Kroslak/K. Kucera (SVK) d. E. Couto/B. Motta (POR) 6–3 6–2 6–2; J. Kroslak (SVK) d. B. Motta (POR) 6–2 6–3; K. Kucera (SVK) d. E. Couto (POR) 6–4 6–1. ● **FINAL** (20-22 SEPTEMBER) - Great Britain d. Egypt 5-0, Wimbledon GBR: G. Rusedski (GBR) d. T. El Sawy (EGY) 6–2 6–4 7–5; T. Henman (GBR) d. A. Ghoneim (EGY) 6–0 6–4 7–5; N. Broad/M. Petchey (GBR) d. T. El Sawy/A. Ghoneim (EGY) 3–6 6–4 6–3 6–4; T. Henman (GBR) d. T. El Sawy (EGY) 6–7(4) 6–2 6–2; G. Rusedski (GBR) d. A. Ghoneim (EGY) 6–4 6–2. Slovak Republic d. Poland 4-1, Trnava SVK: J. Kroslak (SVK) d. B. Dabrowski (POL) 7–6(7) 6–3 6–3; K. Kucera (SVK) d. A. Skzypczak (POL) 6–1 6–1 6–1; J. Kroslak/K. Kucera (SVK) d. M. Chmela/M. Gawlowski (POL) 6–1 6–4 6–7(5) 6–0; K. Kucera (SVK) d. B. Dabrowski (POL) 6–7(2) 6–3 6–4; M. Gawlowski (POL) d. D. Hrbaty (SVK) 6–7(1) 6–3 7–5. Great Britain and Slovak Republic were promoted to Euro/African Group I for the 1997 competition. ● **RELEGATION ROUND** (12-14 JULY) - Slovenia d. Malta 5-0, Novo Mesto SLO: B. Urh (SLO) d. M. Schembri (MLT) 6-0 6-0 6–1; I. Bozic (SLO) d. M. Cappello (MLT) 6-0 6–1 6–1; A. Krasevec/G. Krusic (SLO) d. M. Cappello/M. Schembri (MLT) 6–1 6–3 6–2; I. Bozic (SLO) d. M. Schembri (MLT) 6–1 6–1; B. Urh (SLO) d. M. Cappello (MLT) 6–2 6–1. Latvia d. FYR of Macedonia 3-2, Skopje FYO of Macedonia: A. Filimonovs (LAT) d. O. Nikolovski (MKD) 6–2 6–3 6–1; Z. Sevcenko (MKD) d. G. Dzelde (LAT) 6–3 6–2 1–6 6–1; G. Dzelde/A. Filimonovs (LAT) d. Z. Sevcenko/G. Popov (MKD) 6–4 6–4 6–4; G. Dzelde (LAT) d. G. Popov (MKD) 6–2 6–3 6–2; Z. Sevcenko (MKD) d. A. Filimonovs (LAT) 7–5 7–5. Yugoslavia d. Algeria 5-0, Novi Sad YUG: S. Muskatirovic (YUG) d. A-H. Hameurlaine (ALG) 6–1 6–2 6–1; N. Zimonjic (YUG) d. N. Hakimi (ALG) 7–6(5) 7–6(5) 6–2; D. Vemic/N. Zimonjic (YUG) d. N. Hakimi/A-H. Hameurlaine (ALG) 7–5 6–4 7–6(5); N. Zimonjic (YUG) d. A-H. Hameurlaine (ALG) 3–6 6–3 6–4; D. Vemic (YUG) d. S. Rais Ali (ALG) 6–2 6–1. Nigeria d. Luxembourg: Luxembourg withdrew and Nigeria given walk-over. Malta, FYR Macedonia, Luxembourg and Algeria were relegated to Euro/African III for the 1997 competition.

● **AMERICAN ZONE** Seeding: Uruguay and Ecuador. ● **FIRST ROUND** (9-11 February) - Uruguay d. Guatemala 5-0, Montevideo URU: F. Dondo (URU) d. F. Samayoa (GUA) 6–2 4–6 6–1 6–1; M. Filippini (URU) d. A. Lenoff (GUA) 6–3 6–2 6–0; M. Filippinni/G. Rodriguez (URU) d. L. P. Chete/F. Samayoa (GUA) 6–1 6–1 6–2; M. Filippini (URU) d. F. Samayoa (GUA) 6–3 6–2; F. Dondo (URU) d. A. Lenoff (GUA) 6–3 6–3. Colombia d. Puerto Rico 5-0, Bogota COL: M. Tobon (COL) d. J. Gonzalez (PUR) 6–2 6–2 7–5; M. Hadad (COL) d. R. Jordan (PUR) 6–0 6–2 6–2; M. Hadad/M. Tobon (COL) d. J. Gonzalez/R. Jordan (PUR) 6–4 7–6(3) 6–7(6) 6–7(5) 6–3; M. Hadad (COL) d. J. Gonzalez (PUR) 6–0 4–6 6–2; M. Tobon (COL) d. R. Jordan (PUR) 6–3 6–4. Cuba d. Paraguay 3-2, Havana CUB: R. Delgado (PAR) d. A. Perez (CUB) 7–6(5) 6–4 6–1; J. Pino (CUB) d. R. Mena (PAR) 6–2 6–3 6–1; J. Pino/A. Perez (CUB) d. R. Delgado/R. Mena (PAR) 6–4 7–5 6–2; J. Pino (CUB) d. R. Delgado (PAR) 6–7(4) 6–4 2–6 6–4 11–9; R. Mena (PAR) d. A. Perez (CUB) 1–6 6–4 6–3. Ecuador d. Barbados 5-0, Guayaquil ECU: L. Morejon (ECU) d. M. Blackman (BAR) 6–7(5) 6–1 6–1 6–2; N. Lapentti (ECU) d. R. Ashby (BAR) 6–2 7–6(2) 6–3; A. Gomez/N. Lapentti (ECU) d. R. Ashby/M. Blackman (BAR) 7–5 6–2 6–1; N. Lapentti (ECU) d. M. Blackman (BAR) 6–1 6–2; L. Morejon (ECU) d. R. Ashby (BAR) 7–6(2) 6–2. ● **SECOND ROUND** (7–5 April) - Uruguay d. Colombia 3-2, Montevideo URU: M. Filippini (URU) d. M. Rincon (COL) 6–4 6–3 6–1; M. Hadad (COL) d. F. Dondo (URU) 6–0 6–2 6–3; M. Hadad/M. Rincon (COL) d. M. Filippini/G. Rodriguez (URU) 6–3 3–6 7–5 6–3; M. Filippini (URU) d. P. Moggio (COL) 6–2 7–5 6–2; F. Dondo (URU) d. M. Rincon (COL) 4–6 6–1 6–2 6–3. Ecuador d. Cuba 3-0, Havana CUB: N. Lapentti (ECU) d. A. Perez (CUB) 6–1 6–0 6–2; L. Morejon (ECU) d. J. Pino (CUB) 4–6 7–6(4) 6–1 3–6 8–6; A. Gomez/N. Lapentti (ECU) d. L. Navarro/J. Pino (CUB) 7–6(3) 6–4 6–4; N. Lapentti (ECU) v J. Pino (CUB) and Luis Morejon (ECU) v Armando Perez (CUB) not played due to rain since the tie was already decided. ● **FINAL** (20-22 SEPTEMBER) - Ecuador d. Uruguay 4-1, Guayaquil ECU: N. Lapentti (ECU) d. F. Dondo (URU) 6–4 7–5 6–1; M. Filippini (URU) d. P. Campana (ECU) 6–2 6–1 6–1; A. Gomez/N. Lapentti (ECU) d. M. Filippini/G. Rodriguez (URU) 6–4 6–3 7–6(2); N. Lapentti (ECU) d. M. Filippini (URU) 6–3 6–4 2–6 6–2; L. Morejon (ECU) d. F. Dondo (URU) 6–4 6–1. Ecuador were promoted to American Group I for the 1997 competition. ● **RELEGATION ROUND** (7–5 April) - Paraguay d. Barbados 5-0, Asuncion PAR: R. Mena (PAR) d. M. Blackman (BAR) 6–4 7–6(3) 6–4; R. Delgado (PAR) d. R. Ashby (BAR) 7–6(2) 6–2 6–2; R. Delgado/R. Mena (PAR) d. M. Blackman/R. Ashby (BAR) 3–6 6–2 7–5 6–2; R. Delgado (PAR) d. D. Williams (BAR) 6–0 6–1; R. Mena (PAR) d. R. Ashby (BAR) 6–4 6–2. (3-5 May) - Puerto Rico d. Guatemala 4-1, Guatemala City GUA: J. Gonzalez (PUR) d. A. Lehnhoff (GUA) 6–4 6–2 6–4; F. Samayoa (GUA) d. R. Jordan (PUR) 6–3

7–6(4) 4–6 3–6 6–2; J. Gonzalez/J. Vissepo (PUR) d. F. Samayoa/L. Valencia (GUA) 6–2 7–5 7–5 3–6 9–7; J. Gonzalez (PUR) d. F. Samayoa (GUA) 6–3 7–6(5) 6–3; R. Jordan (PUR) d. A. Lehnhoff (GUA) 6–2 6–4. Barbados and Guatemala were relegated to American Group III for the 1997 competition.

● **ASIA/OCEANIA ZONE** Seeding: Hong Kong and Uzbekistan. ● **FIRST ROUND** (9-11 February) - Hong Kong d. Sri Lanka 5-0, HKG: J. Hui (HKG) d. M. Weerakoon (SRI) 6–3 6–0 6–2; P. Lui (HKG) d. J. Wijesekera (SRI) 7–5 6–3 6–3; J. Hui/S. So (HKG) d. L. Jayasuriya/J. Wijesekera (SRI) 6–3 6–4 6–1; J. Hui (HKG) d. J. Wijesekera (SRI) 6–4 7–6(5); P. Lui (HKG) d. M. Weerakoon (SRI) 6–0 6–0; Thailand d. Iran 4-1, Bangkok THA: W. Thongkhamchu (THA) d. M. Bahrami (IRI) 6–2 6–4 6–4; T. Srichaphan (THA) d. M-R. Tavakoh (IRI) 6–2 6–1 6–1; N. Srichaphan/W. Samrej (THA) d. M. Bahrami/R. Raziani (IRI) 7–5 7–6(4) 6–3; M. Bahrami (IRI) d. T. Srichaphan (THA) 6–4 6–2; W. Thongkhamchu (THA) d. R. Raziani (IRI) 7–5 6–4. ● **SECOND ROUND** (7–5 April) -Thailand d. Hong Kong 5-0, Bangkok THA: T. Srichaphan (THA) d. J. Hui (HKG) 6–2 6–2 6–2; W. Thongkhamchu (THA) d. L. Pang (HKG) 6–3 6–4 6–3; N. Srichaphan/W. Samrej (THA) d. S. So/G. Foster (HKG) 7–5 6–1 6–3; N. Srichaphan (THA) d. G. Foster (HKG) 6–0 6–4; W. Thongkhamchu (THA) d. J. Hui (HKG) 6–3 6–2. Uzbekistan d. Pakistan 5-0, Peshawar PAK: D. Tomashevich (UZB) d. O. Rashid (PAK) 6–3 6–4 6–1; O. Ogorodov (UZB) d. H. Ul Haq (PAK) 6–3 4–6 6–2 6–3; O. Ogorodov/D. Tomashevich (UZB) d. O. Rashid/H. Ul Haq (PAK) 6–7(4) 6–1 7–6(2) 6–3; O. Ogorodov (UZB) d. O. Rashid (PAK) 7–5 6–1; D. Tomashevich (UZB) d. H. Ul Haq (PAK) 6–3 6–2. ● **FINAL** (20-22 SEPTEMBER) - Uzbekistan d. Thailand 5-0, Tashkent UZB: D. Tomashevich (UZB) d. N. Srichaphan (THA) 6–0 6–3 6–1; O. Ogorodov (UZB) d. T. Srichaphan (THA) 6–1 6–3 7–6(2); O. Ogorodov/D. Tomashevich (UZB) d. W. Samrej/W. Thongkhamchu (THA) 6–3 6–4 6–2; O. Ogorodov (UZB) d. N. Srichaphan (THA) 6–3 5–7 6–3; D. Tomashevich (UZB) d. T. Srichaphan (THA) 6–0 6–3. Uzbekistan were promoted to Asia/Oceania Group I for the 1997 competition. ● **RELEGATION ROUND** (7–5 April) - Iran d. Sri Lanka 4-1, Tehran IRI: M. Bahrami (IRI) d. R. de Silva (SRI) 6–2 6–1 7–5; M-R. Tavakoli (IRI) d. J. Wijeyesekera (SRI) 6–2 6–2 6–2; M. Bahrami/R. Raziani (IRI) d. A. Fernando/J. Wijeyesekera (SRI) 6–4 6–2 6–4; J. Wijeyesekera (SRI) d. R. Raziani (IRI) 6–4 6–2; M-R. Tavakoli (IRI) d. R. de Silva (SRI) 6–0 6–2. Saudi Arabia defeated Bahrain 3-2, Riyadh KSA: B. Al-Megayel (KSA) d. Shehab Rashid Shehab (BRN) 6–1 6–2 6–4; O. Al-Anazi (KSA) d. E. Abdul-Aal (BRN) 1–6 2–6 7–6(5) 6–4 6–4; E. Abdul-Aal/N. Abdul-Aal (BRN) d. B. Al-Megayel/O. Al-Anazi (KSA) 6–3 6–4 7–5 6–3; E. Abdul-Aal (BRN) d. B. Al-Megayel (KSA) 4–6 6–2 6–2 7–5; O. Al-Anazi (KSA) d. Shehab Rashid Shehab (BRN) 6–4 7–5 6–3. Sri Lanka and Bahrain relegated to Asia/Oceania Group III for 1997 competition.

● **GROUP III EURO/AFRICAN ZONE A** Istanbul, Turkey 20-26 May.Teams: Armenia, Azerbaijan, Benin, Bosnia/Herzegovina, Ethiopia, Georgia, Iceland, Liechtenstein, Lithuania, San Marino, Senegal, Sudan, Tunisia, Turkey. ● **GROUP A**: Lithuania, Senegal, San Marino, Ethiopia, Azerbaijan, Iceland, Sudan Azerbaijan d. Sudan 2-1: I. Barisov (AZE) d. Abbas Mohammed Ahmed Jeha (SUD) 6–2 6–4; D. Zarubin (AZE) d. Khalid Mohammed Talat Farid (SUD) 7–5 6–1; Asim Omer Abdul-Rahman El Agraa/Khalid Mohammed Talat Farid (SUD) d. E. Kafarov/R. Eyvazov (AZE) 6–2 6–1. San Marino d. Iceland 3-0: M. Rosti (SMR) d. G. Einarsson (ISL) 6–0 7–6(0); D. Vicini (SMR) d. E. Sigurgeirsson (ISL) 6–4 6–3; D. Vicini/C. Rosti (SMR) d. A. Thorbjornsson/S. Palsson (ISL) 7–6(4) 6–4. Senegal d. Ethiopia 2-1: T. Ly (SEN) d. A. Michaile (ETH) 6–4 6–2; A. Berthe (SEN) d. Y. Setegne (ETH) 6–4 6–2; Y. Setegne/A. Michaile (ETH) d. C. Koita/M. Diedhiou (SEN) 4–6 7–6(2) 6–4. Lithuania d. Iceland 3-0: G. Mazonas (LTU) d. S. Palsson (ISL) 6–3 6–1; R. Muraska (LTU) d. A. Thorbjornsson (ISL) 6–1 6–1; D. Ivancovas/E. Cariovas (LTU) d. A. Thorbjornsson/S. Palsson (ISL) 7–6(6) 6–3. Senegal d. Azerbaijan 3-0: T. Ly (SEN) d. D. Zarubin (AZE) 3–6 6–1 6–4; A. Berthe (SEN) d. I. Barisov (AZE) 6–2 6–0; A. Berthe/T. Ly (SEN) d. R. Eyvazov/D. Zarubin (AZE) 6–3 6–3. Ethiopia d. Sudan 2-1: S. Gabriel (ETH) d. Asim Omer Abdul-Rahman El Agraa (SUD) 1–6 6–3 6–1; Y. Setegne (ETH) d. Abbas Mohammed Ahmed Jeha (SUD) 6–1 6–2; Khalid Mohammed Talat Farid/Asim Omer Abdul-Rahman El Agraa (SUD) d. Y. Setegne/A. Michaile (ETH) 1–6 7–5 6–3. Lithuania d. Ethiopia 3-0: G. Mazonas (LTU) d. D. Mebratu (ETH) 6–1 6–0; R. Muraska (LTU) d. S. Gabriel (ETH) 6–2 6–0; D. Ivancovas/E. Cariovas (LTU) d. Y. Setegne/A. Michaile (ETH) 3–6 6–3 6–1. San Marino d. Azerbaijan 3-0: G. Francini (SMR) d. D. Zarubin (AZE) 6–1 6–1; M. Rosti (SMR) d. R. Eyvazov (AZE) 6–0 6–0; D. Vicini/C. Rosti (SMR) d. I. Barisov/R. Eyvazov (AZE) 6–2 7–5 6–1. Iceland d. Sudan 3-0: G. Einarsson (ISL) d. Asim Omer Abdul-Rahman El Agraa (SUD) 6–4 6–1; E. Sigurgeirsson (ISL) d. Khalid Mohammed Talat Farid (SUD) 6–2 6–2; A. Thorbjornsson/G. Einarsson (ISL) d. Khalid Mohammed Talat Farid/Abdulla Nur El Diem (SUD) 6–2 6–3. Lithuania d. San Marino 3-0: G. Mazonas (LTU) d. M. Rosti (SMR) 6–3 7–5; R. Muraska (LTU) d. D. Vicini (SMR) 6–4 6–4; E. Cariovas/D. Ivancovas (LTU) d. G. Francini/D. Vicini (SMR) 6–7(3) 6–3 6–4. Senegal d. Sudan 3-0: T. Ly (SEN) d. Khalid Mohammed Talat Farid (SUD) 6–2 6–4; A. Berthe (SEN) d. Abbas Mohammed Ahmed Jeha (SUD) 6–3 6–1; M. Diedhiou/C. Koita (SEN) d. Abbas Mohammed Ahmed Jeha/Asim Omer Abdul-Rahman El Agraa (SUD) 6–0 2–6 7–5. Ethiopia d. Iceland 2-1: G. Einarsson (ISL) d. A. Michaile (ETH) 6–3 6–1; Y. Setegne (ETH) d. E. Sigurgeirsson (ISL) 6–2 6–2; A. Michaile/Y. Setegne (ETH) d. S. Palsson/A. Thorbjornsson (ISL) 7–5 7–6(4). Lithuania d. Azerbaijan 3-0: E. Cariovas (LTU) d. D. Zarubin (AZE) 4–6 6–2 6–0; R. Muraska (LTU) d. E. Kafarov (AZE) 6–1 6–1; E. Cariovas/R. Muraska (LTU) d. D. Barisov/E. Kafarov (AZE) 6–2 6–1. San Marino d. Sudan 3-0: C. Rosti (SMR) d. Asim Omer Abdul-Rahman El Agraa (SUD) 6–2 6–4; G. Francini (SMR) d. Abbas Mohammed Ahmed Jeha (SUD) 6–1 6–0; M. Rosti/D. Vicini (SMR) d. Asim Omer Abdul-Rahman El Agraa/Abbas Mohammed Ahmed Jeha (SUD) 6–3 6–2. Senegal d. Iceland 3-0: T. Ly (SEN) d. G. Einarsson (ISL) 6–2 6–4; A. Berthe (SEN) d. E. Sigurgeirsson (ISL) 3–6 7–5 6–1; A. Berthe/T. Ly (SEN) d. S. Palsson/E. Sigurgeirsson (ISL) 6–2 6–2. Lithuania d. Sudan 3-0: D. Ivancovas (LTU) d. Asim Omer Abdul-Rahman El Agraa (SUD) 6–2 6–1; G. Mazonas (LTU) d. Abbas Mohammed Ahmed Jeha (SUD) 6–0 6–0; E. Cariovas/D. Ivancovas (LTU) d. Asim Omer Abdul-Rahman El Agraa/Khalid Mohammed Talat Farid (SUD) 6–2 6–2. Ethiopia d. Azerbaijan 3-0: S. Gabriel (ETH) d. D. Zarubin (AZE) 4–6 7–6(7) 6–4; Y. Setegne (ETH) d. I. Barisov (AZE) 6–4 6–3; A. Michaile/Y. Setegne (ETH) d. R. Eyvazov/E. Kafarov (AZE) 6–0 6–2. Senegal d. San Marino 2-1: T. Ly (SEN) d. G. Francini (SMR) 7–5 6–4; D. Vicini (SMR) d. A. Berthe (SEN) 6–7(4) 7–6(6) 13–11; A. Berthe/T. Ly (SEN) d. C. Rosti/M. Rosti (SMR) 6–3 6–4. Lithuania d. Senegal 3-0: G. Mazonas (LTU) d. T. Ly (SEN) 6–0 6–1; R. Muraska (LTU) d. A. Berthe (SEN) 6–1 6–2; E. Cariovas/D. Ivancovas (LTU) d. M. Diedhious/C. Koita (SEN) 7–6(3) 6–3. San Marino d. Ethiopia 3-0: M. Rosti (SMR) d. S. Gabriel (ETH) 6–0 6–1; D. Vicini (SMR) d. Y. Setegne (ETH) 6–4 6–1. Azerbeijan d. Iceland 2-1: D. Zarubin (AZE) d. G. Einarsson (ISL) 1–6 6–4 7–5; I. Borisov (AZE) d. E. Sigurgeirsson (ISL) 4–6 7–6(7) 6–2; A. Thorbjornsson/S. Palsson (ISL) d. I. Borisov/D. Zarubin (AZE) 6–1 6–3. Lithuania were promoted to Euro/African Group II for the 1997 competition.Azerbaijan, Iceland and Sudan were relegated to Euro/African Group IV for the 1997 competition.

● **GROUP B:** Georgia, Turkey, Armenia, Bosnia/Herzegovina, Liechtenstein, Tunisia, BeninTurkey d. Benin 3-0: E. Oral (TUR) d. J-M. da Silva (BEN) 6–4 6–0; M. Azkara (TUR) d. A. Gandonou (BEN) 6–2 6–3; A. Karagoz/B. Ergun (TUR) d. A. Gandonou/J-M. da Silva (BEN) 6–0 6–2. Georgia d. Tunisia 2-1: D. Katcharava (GEO) d. S. Sidia (TUN) 6–4 7–6(4); A. Lahdhiri (TUN) d. V. Gabrichidze (GEO) 4–6 6–3 6–0; V. Margalitadze/D. Katcharava (GEO) d. O. Jallali/S. Sidia (TUN) 6–3 6–4. Armenia d. Bosnia/Herzegovina 2-1: T. Guevorkian (ARM) d. E. Mustafic (BIH) 3–6 6–1 6–4; M. Zahirovic (BIH) d. S. Sargsian (ARM) 6–2 3–6 6–4; S. Sargsian/A. Tpmbakian (ARM) d. M. Zahirovic/H. Basalic (BIH)

6–4 6–4. Georgia d. Armenia 2-1: D. Katcharava (GEO) d. T. Guevorkian (ARM) 6–2 6–2; V. Gabrichidze (GEO) d. S. Sargsjan (ARM) 1–6 6–4 6–4; S. Sargsian/A. Tombakian (ARM) d. V. Margalitadze/I. Kunchula (GEO) 6–2 6–3. Bosnia/Herzegovina d. Tunisia 2-1: E. Mustafic (BIH) d. O. Jallali (TUN) 6–4 6–7(5) 6–2; M. Zahirovic (BIH) d. A. Lahdhiri (TUN) 6–2 6–0; S. Sami/O. Jallali (TUN) d. E. Mustafic/H. Basalic (BIH) 7–5 6–1. Turkey d. Liechtenstein 3-0: B. Ergun (TUR) d. S. Ritter (LIE) 7–5 6–3; A. Karagoz (TUR) d. C. Hoop (LIE) 6–3 7–6(0); M. Azkara/E. Oral (TUR) d. J. Tomordy/D. Kieber (LIE) 6–3 6–2. Georgia d. Benin 3-0: D. Katcharava (GEO) d. C. Pognon (BEN) 6–3 6–3; V. Margalitadze (GEO) d. A. Gandonou (BEN) 6–1 6–2; V. Margalitadze/I. Kunchula (GEO) d. T. Gandonou/J-M. da Silva (BEN) 6–3 6–2. Armenia d. Liechtenstein 3-0: T. Guervorkian (ARM) d. D. Kieber (LIE) 6–2 6–2; S. Sargsjan (ARM) d. J. Tomordy (LIE) 6–0 6–0; S. Sargsjan/A. Tombakian (ARM) d. C. Hoop/S. Ritter (LIE) 6–3 6–1. Turkey d. Bosnia/Herzegovina 2-1: E. Oral (TUR) d. E. Mustafic (BIH) 7–6(4) 6–1; M. Zahirovic (BIH) d. A. Karagoz (TUR) 7–5 6–4; M. Azkara/E. Oral (TUR) d. E. Mustafic/M. Zahirovic (BIH) 7–5 6–1. Liechtenstein d. Benin 2-1: S. Ritter (LIE) d. C. Pognon (BEN) 6–3 6–0; C. Hoop (LIE) d. A. Gandonou (BEN) 7–6(5) 6–3; A. Gandonou/J-M. da Silva (BEN) d. J. Tomordy/D. Kieber (LIE) 7–6(4) 6–3. Armenia d. Tunisia 3-0: T. Guevorkian (ARM) d. S. Sidia (TUN) 6–4 3–6 6–4; S. Sargsian (ARM) d. A. Lahdhiri (TUN) 4–6 6–0 6–1; S. Sargsian/A. Tombakian (ARM) d. O. Jallali/S. Sidia (TUN) 6–1 4–6 6–3. Georgia d. Bosnia/Herzegovina 2-1: V. Margalitadze (GEO) d. H. Basalic (BIH) 6–3 6–4; M. Zahirovic (BIH) d. V. Gabrichidze (GEO) 6–1 6–3; V. Gabrichidze/D. Katcharava (GEO) d. E. Mustafic/M. Zahirovic (BIH) 6–4 6–0. Bosnia/Herzegovina d. Liechtenstein 2-1: S. Ritter (LIE) d. E. Mustafic (BIH) 1–6 6–4 6–4; M. Zahirovic (BIH) d. C. Hoop (LIE) 6–3 4–6 6–1; E. Mustafic/M. Zahirovic (BIH) d. C. Hoop/S. Ritter (LIE) 6–1 4–6 6–3. Tunisia d. Benin 2-1: O. Jallali (TUN) d. C. Pognon (BEN) 6–1 1–6 8–6; A. Lahdhiri (TUN) d. A. Gandonou (BEN) 7–6(3) 6–3; A. Gandonou/J-M. da Silva (BEN) d. O. Jallali/H. Kastalli (TUN) 7–5 6–3. Turkey d. Armenia 2-1: E. Oral (TUR) d. T. Guevorkian (ARM) 7–5 6–3; S. Sargsian (ARM) d. M. Azkara (TUR) 6–1 6–1; A. Karagoz/B. Ergun (TUR) d. S. Sargsian/A. Tombakian (ARM) 6–3 7–6(2). Liechtenstein d. Tunisia 3-0: S. Ritter (LIE) d. H. Kastalli (TUN) 6–4 6–0; C. Hoop (LIE) d. O. Jallali (TUN) 6–2 7–5; D. Kieber/J. Tomordy (LIE) d. O. Jallali/H. Kastalli (TUN) 6–3 4–6 6–4. Armenia d. Benin 2-1: C. Pognon (BEN) d. A. Nesisian (ARM) 7–5 4–6 6–1; T. Guervokian (ARM) d. A. Gandonou (BEN) 6–2 6–4; T. Guervokian/S. Sargsian (ARM) d. A. Gandonou/J-M. da Silva (BEN) 6–1 6–0. Georgia d. Turkey 2-1: D. Katcharava (GEO) d. E. Oral (TUR) 6–0 7–5(5); A. Karagoz (TUR) d. V. Gabrichidze (GEO) 6–4 3–6 7–5; V. Gabrichidze/D. Katcharava (GEO) d. B. Ergun/A. Karagoz (TUR) 6–2 6–2. Bosnia/Herzegovina d. Benin 3-0: E. Mustafic (BIH) d. T. Gandonou (BEN) 6–0 6–0; M. Zahirovic (BIH) d. A. Gandonou (BEN) 6–1 6–2; E. Mustafic/M. Zahirovic (BIH) d. A. Gandonou/T. Gandonou (BEN) 6–1 6–1. Turkey d. Tunisia 3-0: E. Oral (TUR) d. H. Kastalli (TUN) 6–3 6–0; M. Azkara (TUR) d. O. Jallali (TUN) 6–2 6–4; M. Azkara/E. Oral (TUR) d. O. Jallali/H. Kastalli (TUN) 6–0 6–3. Georgia d. Liechtenstein 2-1: S. Ritter (LIE) d. I. Kunchula (GEO) 7–6(6) 6–0; V. Margalitadze (GEO) d. C. Hoop (LIE) 7–6(5) 6–3; V. Gabrichidze/V. Margalitadze (GEO) d. J. Tomordy/S. Ritter (LIE) 6–2 6–2. Georgia were promoted to Euro/African Group II for the 1997 competition. Liechtenstein, Tunisia and Benin were relegated to Euro/African Group IV for the 1997 competition.

● **EURO/AFRICAN ZONE B** Nairobi, Kenya, 8 - 14 January. Teams: Botswana, Bulgaria, Cameroun, Congo, Cyprus, Djibouti, Estonia, Greece, Ireland, Kenya, Moldova, Monaco, Togo and Zambia. ● **GROUP A:** Cameroun, Djibouti, Cyprus, Estonia, Ireland, Moldova, Zambia. Estonia d. Moldova 2–1: E. Plougarev (MDA) d. A. Hint (EST) 3–6 2–6; R. Busch (EST) d. O. Sinic (MDA) 6–0 6–2; A. Luzgin/A. Vahkal (EST) d. E. Plougarev/M. Savitski (MDA) 6–0 6–7(8) 6–3. Cyprus d. Zambia 3–0: A. Papamichael (CYP) d. K. Sinkala (ZAM) 6–3 6–0; D. Leondis (CYP) d. S. Bwalya (ZAM) 7–5 6–3; D. Leondis/A. Morfiadakis (CYP) d. M. Kombe/L. Ndefway (ZAM) 7–6(9) 6–4. Ireland d Djibouti 3–0: S. Barron (IRL) d. A. Abdul-Nasser (DJI) 6–1 6–0; O. Casey (IRL) d. C. Nasser-Saeed (DJI) 6–2 6–0; E. Collins/J. Doran (IRL) d. A. Abdul-Nasser/A. Aden (DJI) 6–0 6–0. Moldova d. Cyprus 2–1: E. Plougarev (MDA) d. A. Papamichael (CYP) 6–3 6–1; O. Sinic (MDA) d. D. Leondis (CYP) 6–4 6–1; D. Leondis/A. Morfiadakis (CYP) d. S. Bougaenko/E. Plougarev (MDA) 2–6 2–6. Zambia d. Djibouti 3–0: K. Sinkala (ZAM) d. A. Aden (DJI) 6–0 6–0; S. Bwalya (ZAM) d. C. Nasser-Saeed (DJI) 6–1 6–0; M. Kombe/L. Ndefway (ZAM) d. A. Abdul-Nasser/C. Nasser-Saeed (DJI) 6–1 6–3. Cameroun d. Estonia 2–1: A. Mvogo (CMR) d. A. Hint (EST) 6–1 6–1; R. Busch (EST) d. L. Kemajou (CMR) 2–6 0–6; A. Mvogo/J. Oyebog (CMR) d. A. Luzgin/A. Vahkal (EST) 7–6(5) 6–4. Ireland d. Cyprus 3–0: S. Barron (IRL) d. A. Morfiadakis (CYP) 6–2 6–1; O. Casey (IRL) d. A. Papamichael (CYP) 6–1 6–4; O. Casey/E. Collins (IRL) d. D. Leondis/A. Morfiadakis (CYP) 5–2 ret. Cameroun d. Moldova 2–1: A. Mvogo (CMR) d. E. Plougarev (MDA) 6–4 6–3; O. Sinic (MDA) d. L. Kemajou (CMR) 4–6 4–6; A. Mvogo/J. Oyebog (CMR) d. M. Savitski/O. Sinic (MDA) 6–3 6–7(7) 6–1. Estonia d. Zambia 3–0: A. Vahkal (EST) d. K. Sinkala (ZAM) 6–0 6–4; R. Busch (EST) d. S. Bwalya (ZAM) 6–2 6–1; A. Luzgin/A. Vahkal (EST) d. M. Kombe/L. Ndefway (ZAM) 6–4 6–2. Estonia d. Djibouti 3–0: A. Vahkal (EST) d. A. Abdul-Nasser (DJI) 6–3 6–1; R. Busch (EST) d. C. Nasser-Saeed (DJI) 6–2 6–0; A. Hint/A. Luzgin (EST) d. A. Abdul-Nasser/A. Aden (DJI) 6–1 6–1. Ireland d. Cameroun 2–1: A. Mvogo (CMR) d. S. Barron (IRL) 4–6 1–6; O. Casey (IRL) d. L. Kemajou (CMR) 6–1 6–2; O. Casey/E. Collins (IRL) d. A. Mvogo/J.Oyebog (CMR) 6–4 6–2. Moldova d. Zambia 2–1: K. Sinkala (ZAM) d. E. Plougarev (MDA) 4–6 3–6; O. Sinic (MDA) d. S. Bwalya (ZAM) 6–4 6–3; M. Savitski/O. Sinic (MDA) d. S. Bwalya/K. Sinkala (ZAM) 2–6 6–3 6–4. Moldova d. Djibouti 3–0: E. Plougarev (MDA) d. A. Abdul-Nasser (DJI) 6–1 6–3; O. Sinic (MDA) d. N. Chamsan (DJI) 6–1 6–1; E. Plougarev/O. Sinic (MDA) d. A. Abdul-Nasser/C. Nasser Saeed (DJI) 6–0 6–1. Cameroun d. Cyprus 2–1: J. Oyebog (CMR) d. A. Papamichael (CYP) 6–3 3–6 11–13; A. Mvogo (CMR) d. D. Leondis (CYP) 6–2 6–4; D. Leondis/A. Morfiadakis (CYP) d. M. Fomete/L. Kemajou (CMR) 2–6 3–6. Ireland d. Zambia 3–0: S. Barron (IRL) d. K. Sinkala (ZAM) 6–3 6–4; O. Casey (IRL) d. S. Bwalya (ZAM) 6–1 6–0; S. Barron/O.Casey (IRL) d. M. Kombe/L. Ndefway (ZAM) 6–1 6–1. Cameroun d. Djibouti 3–0: J. Oyebog (CMR) d. A. Aden (DJI) 6–0 6–0; L. Kemajou (CMR) d. A. Abdul-Nasser (DJI) 6–1 6–0; M. Fomete/A. Mvogo (CMR) d. A. Abdul-Nasser/A. Aden (DJI) 6–1 6–1. Estonia d. Cyprus 3–0: A. Vahkal (EST) d. A. Papamichael (CYP) 6–4 6–7(4) 6–3; R. Busch (EST) d. D. Leondis (CYP) 6–4 4–6 6–2; A. Luzgin/A. Vahkal (EST) d. P. Baghdatis/A. Morfiadakis (CYP) 6–1 6–3. Ireland d. Moldova 3–0: S. Barron (IRL) d. E. Plougarev (MDA) 6–2 6–3; O. Casey (IRL) d. O. Sinic (MDA) 7–5 3–6 6–3; O. Casey/E. Collins (IRL) d. M. Savitski/O. Sinic (MDA) 6–4 6–2. Ireland d. Estonia 3–0: S. Barron (IRL) d. A. Hint (EST) 6–0 6–0; O. Casey (IRL) d. R. Busch (EST) 6–1 6–2; S. Barron/J. Doran (IRL) d. A. Luzgin/A. Vahkal (EST) 4–6 6–4 6–3. Cyprus d. Djibouti 3–0: A. Morfiadakis (CYP) d. A. Aden (DJI) 6–0 6–0; D. Leondis (CYP) d. A. Abdul-Nasser (DJI) 6–1 6–2; P.Baghdatis/D. Leondis (CYP) d. A.Abdul-Nasser/C. Nasser-Saeed (DJI) 6–0 6–1. Cameroun d. Zambia 3–0: A. Mvogo (CMR) d. K. Sinkala (ZAM) 6–2 6–3; L. Kemajou (CMR) d. S. Bwalya (ZAM) 6–1 6–4; M. Fomete/L. Kemajou (CMR) d. M. Kombe/L. Ndefway (ZAM) 7–5 6–1. Ireland were promoted to Euro/African Group II for the 1997 competition. Cyrus, Zambia and Djibouti were relegated to Euro/African Group IV for the 1997 competition.

● **GROUP B:** Botswana, Bulgaria, Congo, Greece, Kenya, Monaco, Togo. Kenya d. Botswana 3–0: N. Odour (KEN) d. M. Judd (BOT) 6–1 6–4; A. Cooper (KEN) d. G. Jeftha (BOT) 6–4 6–2; A. Cooper/N. Odour (KEN) d. G. Jeftha/T. Kgosimore (BOT) 6–2 6–1: Greece d. Togo 3–0: K. Efremolglou (GRE) d. K. Akli (TOG) 6–2 6–1; S. Peppas (GRE) d. Komi Loglo (TOG) 6–3 6–4; C. Economidis/N. Rovas (GRE) d. K. Akli/Komi Loglo (TOG) 4–6 6–3 6–4. Bulgaria d. Monaco 3–0: R. Raynov (BUL) d. C. Bosio (MON) 4–6 6–3 6–1; M. Markov (BUL) d. S. Graeff (MON)

6–4 6–4; I. Bratanov/R. Radev (BUL) d. C. Boggetti/S. Graeff (MON) 6–1 7–6(6). Monaco d. Greece 2–1: K. Efremoglou (GRE) d. C. Bosio (MON) 3–6 4–6; S. Graeff (MON) d. S. Peppas (GRE) 4–6 6–4 6–2; C. Boggeti/S. Graeff (MON) d. K. Efremoglou/S. Peppas (GRE) 7–6(6) 7–6(3). Bulgaria d. Botswana 3–0: R. Radev (BUL)d. G. Jeftha (BOT) 6–4 6–3; M. Markov (BUL) d. T. Kgosimore (BOT) 6–1 6–4; I. Bratanov/R. Radev (BUL) d. M. Judd/T. Kgosimore (BOT) 6–4 6–4. Togo d. Congo 3–0: K. Akli (TOG) d. C. Gnitou (CGO) 6–4 6–1; Komi Loglo (TOG) d. A. Bemba (CGO) 6–0 6–2; Kossi Loglo/K. Sodji (TOG) d. A. Bemba/C. Gnitou (CGO) 7–5 6–3. Bulgaria d. Kenya 3–0: R. Raynov (BUL) d. N. Odour (KEN) 1–6 6–3 6–4; M. Markov (BUL) d. A. Cooper (KEN) 6–3 1–6 7–5; I. Bratanov/R. Radev (BUL) d. A. Balaraman/D. Shretta (KEN) 6–7(5) 6–3 7–5. Monaco d. Congo 3–0: C. Bosio (MON) d. M. Banguid (CGO) 6–2 6–2; S. Graeff (MON) d. C. Gnitou (CGO) 6–3 6–0; C. Boggetti/S. Skudlarek (MON) d. M. Banguid/A. Bemba (CGO) 6–1 6–2. Greece d. Botswana 3–0: K. Economidis (GRE) d. T. Kgosimore (BOT) 6–2 6–1; S. Peppas (GRE) d. M. Judd (BOT) 6–3 6–4; K. Efremoglou/N. Rovas (GRE) d. G. Jeftha/M. Judd (BOT) 6–2 6–2. Greece d. Kenya 3–0: K. Efremoglou (GRE) d. A. Balamaran (KEN) 6–0 6–2; S. Peppas (GRE) d. A. Cooper (KEN) 6–3 6–4; K. Efremoglou/S. Peppas (GRE) d. A. Cooper/N. Odour (KEN) 2–6 7–6(7) 6–4. Botswana d. Congo 3–0: M. Judd (BOT) d. M. Banguid (CGO) 6–3 6–1; G. Jeftha (BOT) d. C. Gnitou (CGO) 6–2 6–4; M. Judd/T. Kgosimore (BOT) d. A. Bemba/C. Gnitou (CGO) 6–2 6–4. Monaco d. Togo 3–0: C. Bosio (MON) d. K. Akli (TOG) 6–4 6–0; S. Graeff (MON) d. Komi Loglo (TOG) 7–6(4) 7–6(0); C. Bogetti/S. Skudlarek (MON) d. Kossi Loglo/K. Sodji (TOG) 6–3 6–4. Greece d. Bulgaria 3–0: C. Efremoglou (GRE) d. R. Raynov (BUL) 7–6(6) 6–3; S. Peppas (GRE) d. M. Markov (BUL) 7–6(6) 2–6 7–5; C. Efremoglou/S. Peppas (GRE) d. M. Markov/R. Radev (BUL) 6 2 6 3. Kenya d. Congo 3–0: N. Odour (KEN) d. M. Banguid (CGO) 6–0 6–2; A. Cooper (KEN) d. C. Gnitou (CGO) 6–1 6–2; A. Cooper/N. Odour (KEN) d. M. Banguid/A. Bemba (CGO) 6–2 6–0. Botswana d. Togo 3–0: M. Judd (BOT) d. K. Akli (TOG) 6–4 6–7(3) 8–6; G. Jeftha (BOT) d. Komi Loglo (TOG) 6–2 6–4; M. Judd/T. Kgosimore (BOT) d. Kossi Loglo/K. Sodji (TOG) 7–6(6) 6–3. Kenya d. Togo 3–0: R. Odour (KEN) d. Kossi Loglo (TOG) 4–6 6–2 6–2; A. Cooper (KEN) d. Komi Loglo (TOG) 2–6 6–4 6–3; A. Balaraman/D. Shretta (KEN) d. Komi Loglo/Kossi Loglo (TOG) 6–2 7–6(9). Bulgaria d. Congo 3–0: R. Radev (BUL) d. M. Banguid (CGO) 6–0 6–1; I. Bratanov d. (BUL) A. Bemba (CGO) 6–1 6–3; I. Bratanov/R. Radev (BUL) d. M. Banguid/C. Gnitou (CGO) 6–0 6–3. Monaco d. Botswana 3–0: S. Skudlarek (MON) d. M. Judd (BOT) 6–3 7–6(3); C. Boggetti (MON) d. G. Jeftha (BOT) 6–3 6–7(8) 6–0. C. Bosio/S. Graeff (MON) d. M. Judd/T. Kgosimore (BOT) 6–7(5) 7–6(4) 18–16. Monaco d. Kenya 2–1: N. Odour (KEN) d. S. Skudlarek (MON) 4–6 2–6; S. Graeff (MON) d. A. Cooper (KEN) 7–6(5) 6–7(3) 6–3; S. Boggetti/S. Graeff (MON) d. A. Cooper/N. Odour (KEN) 3–6 3–6 4. Bulgaria d. Togo 3–0: R. Radev (BUL) d. Kossi Loglo (TOG) 6–1 6–2; M. Markov (BUL) d. Komi Loglo (TOG) 7–6(5) 3–0 ret; M. Markov/R. Radev (BUL) d. K. Akli/Kossi Loglo (TOG) 6–2 6–3. Greece d. Congo 3–0: C. Efremoglou (GRE) d. M. Banguid (CGO) 6–0 6–0; S. Peppas (GRE) d. C. Gnitou (CGO) 6–1 6–1; C. Economidis/N. Rovas (GRE) d. A. Bemba/C. Ossombi-Mayela (CGO) 6–2 6–0. Greece were promoted to Euro/African Group II for the 1997 competition. Botswana, Togo and Congo were relegated to Euro/African Group IV for the 1997 competition.

● **AMERICAN ZONE** Maya Country Club, San Salvador, El Salvador, 4 – 10 MarchTeams: Antigua and Barbuda, Bermuda, Bolivia, Costa Rica, Dominican Republic, El Salvador, Haiti, Jamaica, OECS, Panama, Trinidad and Tobago. ● **GROUP A:** Antigua and Barbuda, Costa Rica, Dominican Republic, Haiti, Trinidad and Tobago. Haiti d. Costa Rica 3–0: B. Madsen (HAI) d. F. Golfin (CRC) 6–3 6–2; R. Agenor (HAI) d. R. Avalos (CRC) 6–3 6–2; B. Lacombe/B. Madsen (HAI) d. A. Arias/F. Golfin (CRC) 6–1, 6–3. Dominican Republic d. Trinidad and Tobago 3-0: R. Vallejo (DOM) d. E. Campbell (TRI) 6–1 6–1; H. Silfa (DOM) d. S. Evelyn (TRI) 6–0 6–3; A. Aybar/S. Camacho (DOM) d. O. Adams/S. Evelyn (TRI) 7–6(5) 6–3. Dominican Republic d. Antigua and Barbuda 2–1: R. Vallejo (DOM) d. J. Williams (ANT) 6–4 6–4; P. Williamson (ANT) d. H. Silfa (DOM) 3–6 1–6; S. Camacho/H. Silfa (DOM) d. J. Williams/P. Williamson (ANT) 6–4 7–5. Trinidad and Tobago d. Costa Rica 2–1: F. Martinez (CRC) d. E. Campbell (TRI) 2–6 3–6; S. Evelyn (TRI) d. F. Golfin (CRC) 2–6 7–6(2), 6–4; O. Adams/S. Evelyn (TRI) d. A. Arias/R. Avalos (CRC) 3–6 6–3 6–3. Trinidad and Tobago d. Antigua and Barbuda 2–1: O. Adams (TRI) d. J. Williams (ANT) 6–3 6–1; P. Williamson (ANT) d. S. Evelyn (TRI) 4–6 2–6; O. Adams/S. Evelyn (TRI) d. E. Browne/P. Williamson (ANT) 6–4 6–7(6) 6–3. Haiti d. Dominican Republic 3–0: B. Madsen (HAI) d. R. Vallejo (DOM) 7–5 6–3; R. Agenor (HAI) d. H. Silfa (DOM) 6–4 3–6 7–5; B. Lacombe/B. Madsen (HAI) d. A. Aybar/S. Camacho (DOM) 6–3 6–3. Antigua and Barbuda d. Costa Rica 3–0: J. Williams (ANT) d. F. Martinez (CRC) 6–1 4–6 6–2; P. Williamson (ANT) d. R. Avalos (CRC) 2–6 6–2 6–4; F. Anthony/E. Browne (ANT) d. A. Arias/F. Martinez (CRC) 6–4 6–4. Haiti d. Trinidad and Tobago 3–0: B. Madsen (HAI) d. O. Adams (TRI) 6–2 6–3; R. Agenor (HAI) d. S. Evelyn (TRI) 6–4 6–0; B. Lacombe/B. Madsen (HAI) d. E. Campbell/R. Greaves (TRI) 6–1 6–3. Haiti d. Antigua and Barbuda 3–0: B. Madsen (HAI) d. J. Williams (ANT) 6–2 7–5; R. Agenor (HAI) d. P. Williamson (ANT) 6–3 6–3; R. Goscinny/B. Lacombe (HAI) d. F. Anthony/E. Browne (ANT) 7–6(2) 6–4. Dominican Republic d. Costa Rica 3–0: R. Vallejo (DOM) d. A. Arias (CRC) 6–4 6–1; H. Silfa (DOM) d. F. Golfin (CRC) 6–4 6–4; A. Aybar/S. Camacho (DOM) d. R. Avalos/F. Golfin (CRC) 6–7(3) 6–4 6–2. Haiti were promoted to American Group II for the 1997 competition. Costa Rica were relegated to American Group IV for the 1997 competition.

● **GROUP B:** Bermuda, Bolivia, El Salvador, Jamaica, Panama, OECS Jamaica d. Bolivia 2–1: P. Ugarte (BOL) d. S. Willinsky (JAM) 5–7 3–6; N. Malcolm (JAM) d. C. Navarro (BOL) 7–6(5) 6–1; N. Malcolm/S. Willinsky (JAM) d. C. Navarro/P. Ugarte (BOL) 6–2 3–6 7–5. Panama d. Bermuda 2–1: J-P. Herrera (PAN) d. J. Collieson (BER) 6–3 6–4; M. Way (BER) d. C. Silva (PAN) 1–6 6–2 4–6; G. Garibaldi/J. Gelabert (PAN) d. S. Bean/R. Mallory (BER) 6–4 6–1. El Salvador d. OECS 3–0: M.Tejada (ESA) d. K. Easter (ECA) 6–2 6–2; M. Merz (ESA) d. H. Sinson (ECA) 6–2 6–0; M. Merz/M. Tejada (ESA) d. K. Cable/R. Hughes (ECA) 7–6(1) 7–5. El Salvador d. Bermuda 3–0: M. Tejada (ESA) d. M. Way (BER) 6–0 6–3; M. Merz (ESA) d. R. Mallory (BER) 6–3 6–2; M. Merz/M. Tejada (ESA) d. S. Bean/J. Collieson (BER) 6–3 6–0. Jamaica d. OECS 2–1: K. Easter (ECA) d. P. Gordon (JAM) 6–7(12) 4–6; N. Malcolm (JAM) d. H. Sinson (ECA) 7–5 6–3; N. Malcolm/S. Willinsky (JAM) d. K. Easter/H. Sinson (ECA) 6–2 6–3. Panama d. Bolivia 2–1: J-P. Herrera (PAN) d. P. Ugarte (BOL) 6–2 7–6(5); C. Navarro (BOL) d. C. Silva (PAN) 6–7(3) 6–2 4–6; G. Garibaldi/J. Gelabert (PAN) d. C. Navarro/P. Ugarte (BOL) 6–4 7–5. El Salvador d. Panama 3–0: M. Tejada (ESA) d. J. Gelabert (PAN) 6–3 6–1; M. Merz (ESA) d. J-P. Herrera (PAN) 6–4 6–4; M. Merz/M. Tejada (ESA) d. G. Garibalid/J. Gelabert (PAN) 6–1 7–5. Jamaica d. Bermuda 3–0: S. Willinsky (JAM) d. M. Way (BER) 7–5 6–7(2) 7–5; N. Malcolm (JAM) d. R. Mallory (BER) 6–1 6–1; P. Gordon/E. Henry (JAM) d. J. Collieson/R. Mallory (BER) 5–7 6–3 6–3. Bolivia d. OECS 3–0: E. Kohlberg (BOL) d. K. Easter (ECA) 7–5 6–2; C. Navarro (BOL) d. H. Sinson (ECA) 6–2 6–3; E. Kohlberg/M. Quiroga (BOL) d. K. Easter/R. Hughes (ECA) 6–4 6–1. El Salvador d. Jamaica 2–1: M. Tejada (ESA) d. S. Willinsky (JAM) 7–6(5) 6–4; M. Merz (ESA) d. N. Malcolm (JAM) 6–1 6–4; N. Malcolm/S. Willinsky (JAM) d. J. Baires/R. Fuentes (ESA) 4–6 3–6. Bolivia d. Bermuda 3–0: P. Ugarte (BOL) d. J. Collieson (BER) 6–4 6–2; C. Navarro (BOL) d. M. Way (BER) 6–3 6–4; E. Kohlberg/M. Quiroga (BOL) d. S. Bean/R. Mallory (BER) 6–2 6–4. Panama d. OECS 2–1: J-P. Herrera (PAN) d. K. Easter (ECA) 3–6 6–4 6–1; C. Silva (PAN) d. H. Sinson (ECA) 7–6(4) 6–4; K. Cable/R. Hughes (ECA) d. G. Garibaldi/ J-P. Herrera (PAN) 7–5 5–7 9–11. El Salvador d. Bolivia 3–0: M. Tejada (ESA) d. E. Kohlberg (BOL) 6–3 6–2; M. Merz (ESA) d. C. Navarro (BOL) 6–3 4–6 8–6; R. Fuente/M. Merz (ESA) d.

C. Navarro/P. Ugarte (BOL) 6–4 6–2. Bermuda d. OECS 2–1: K. Easter (ECA) d. J. Collieson (BER) 1–6 3–6; M. Way (BER) d. H. Sinson (ECA) 3–6 7–6(2) 8–6; R. Mallory/M. Way (BER) d. K. Cable/R. Hughes (ECA) 5–7 6–0 6–4. Panama d. Jamaica 3–0: J-P. Herrera (PAN) d. S. Willinsky (JAM) 7–5 7–6(5); C. Silva (PAN) d. N. Malcolm (JAM) 6–3 0–6 6–0; G. Garibaldi/J-P. Herrera (PAN) d. P. Gordon/A. Henry (JAM) 7–5 6–4. El Salvador were promoted to American Group II for the 1997 competition. Bermuda and OECS were relegated to American Group IV for the 1997 competition.

● **ASIA/OCEANIA ZONE** Dubai, United Arab Emirates, 18-24 March Teams: Kazakhstan, Malaysia, Oman, Pacific Oceania, Singapore, Syria, Bangladesh, Brunei Darussalam, Jordan, Kuwait, Lebanon, Qatar United Arab Emirates. GROUP A: Kazakhstan, Malaysia, Oman, Pacific Oceania, Singapore and Syria. Singapore d. Syria 2–1: C-Y. Chen (SIN) d. M. Al-Amin (SYR) 6–1 6–1; R. Bou-Hassoun (SYR) d. Y-T. Lim (SIN) 7 6(3) 6 2; J M. Lam/Y-T. Lim (SIN) d. R. Bou Hassoun/D. Dawoodian (SYR) 6–2 6–4. Malaysia d. Kazakhstan 2-1: J-G. Chua (MAS) d. D. Arissov (KAZ) 3–6 6–4 6–2; A. Kedriouk (KAZ) d. V. Ortchuan (MAS) 7 5 2 6 6–4; J-G. Chua/A-A. Shazali (MAS) d. D. Arissov/I. Chaldounov (SYR) 6–3 6–3. Pacific Oceania d. Oman 2-1: L. Tenai (POC) d. B. Al-Sharji (OMA) 6–2 6–0; M. Al-Rawahi (OMA) d. S. Tikaram (POC) 6–2 7–5; L. Tenai/S. Tikaram (POC) d. M. Al-Rawahi/B. Al-Sharji (OMA) 6–2 6–2. Singapore d. Pacific Oceania 2-1: L. Tenai (POC) d. J-M. Lam (SIN) 7–5 6–4; C-Y. Chen (SIN) d. S. Tikaram (POC) 7–6(3) 6–0; J-M. Lam/Y-T. Lim (SIN) d. L. Tenai/S. Tikaram (POC) 7–5 6–3 6–4. Malaysia d. Oman 2-1: V. Ortchuan (MAS) d. B. Al-Sharji (OMA) 6–1 6–0; M. Al-Rawahi (OMA) d. H-K. Cheng (MAS) 6–1 6–0; J-G. Chua/A-A. Shazali (MAS) d. M. Al-Rawahi/B. Al-Sharji (OMA) 6–0 6–2. Kazakhstan d. Syria 2-1: D. Arissov (KAZ) d. D. Dawoodian (SYR) 6–2 3–6 6–4; R. Bou-Hassoun (SYR) d. A. Kedriouk (KAZ) 3–6 6–1 6–2; M. Al-Amin/R. Bou-Hassoun (SYR) d. I. Chaldounov/A. Kedriouk (KAZ) 2–6 6–0 7–5. Singapore d. Kazakhstan 2-1: C-Y. Chen (SIN) d. I. Chaldounov (KAZ) 6–2 6–2; D. Arissov (KAZ) d. Y-T. Lim (SIN) 6–3 7–6(2); J-M. Lam/Y-T. Lim (SIN) d. D. Arissov/A. Kedriouk (KAZ) 6–3 3–6 6–4. Malaysia d. Pacific Oceania 2-1: A-A. Shazali (MAS) d. H. Morriswala (POC) 6–2 6–2; J-G. Chua (MAS) d. L. Tenai (POC) 7–6(4) 4–6 6–1; C. Mainguy/H. Morriswala (POC) d. H-K. Cheng/V. Ortchuan (MAS) 7–5 7–5 6–4. Syria d. Oman 3-0: D. Dawoodian (SYR) d. B. Al-Sharji (OMA) 6–3 6–0; R. Bou-Hassoun (SYR) d. M. Al-Rawahi (OMA) 2–6 6–2 6–1; D. Dawoodian/L. Salim (SYR) d. M. Al-Rawahi/B. Al-Sharji (OMA) 6–4 7–6(7). Singapore d. Malaysia 3-0: J-M. Lam (SIN) d. A-A. Shazali (MAS) 6–3 6–2; C-Y. Chen (SIN) d. J-G. Chua (MAS) 6–1 7–5; J-M. Lam/Y-T. Lim (SIN) d. J-G. Chua/A-A. Shazali (MAS) 6–2 7–6(4). Pacific Oceania d. Syria 2-1: L. Tenai (POC) d. M. Al-Amin (SYR) 6–1 3–6 6–2; R. Bou-Hassoun (SYR) d. S. Tikaram (POC) 6–0 6–1; L. Tenai/S. Tikaram (POC) d. M. Al-Amin/R. Bou-Hassoun (SYR) 6–3 6–2. Kazakhstan d. Oman 2-1: D. Arissov (KAZ) d. B. Al-Sharji (OMA) 6–1 6–2; M. Al-Rawahi (OMA) d. A. Kedriouk (KAZ) 6–1 3–6 6–2; D. Arissov/I. Chaldounov (KAZ) d. M. Al-Rawahi/B. Al-Sharji (OMA) 6–1 6–2. Singapore d. Oman 2-1: J-M. Lam (SIN) d. B. Al-Sharji (OMA) 6–3 6–2; M. Al-Rawahi (OMA) d. C-Y. Chen (SIN) 3–6 6–2 6–3; K-H. Lim/Y-T. Lim (SIN) d. F. Al-Hashmi/M. Al-Rawahi (OMA) 6–2 6–1. Syria d. Malaysia 2-1: D. Dawoodian (SYR) d. V. Ortchuan (MAS) 6–3 6–4; R. Bou-Hassoun (SYR) d. H-K Cheng (MAS) 6–3 3–6 7–5; J-G. Chua/A-A. Shazali (MAS) d. D. Dawoodian/L. Salim (SYR) 7–5 1–6 6–2. Pacific Oceania d. Kazakhstan 2-1: L. Tenai (POC) d. D. Arissov (KAZ) 6–3 6–4; S. Tikaram (POC) d. A. Kedriouk (KAZ) 6–4 6–4; I. Chaldounov/A. Kedriouk (KAZ) defeated C. Mainguy/H. Morriswala (POC) 3–6 6–4 6–3. Singapore were promoted to Asia/Oceania Group II for the 1997 competition. Syria and Oman were relegated to Asia/Oceania Group IV for the 1997 competition. ● **GROUP B:** Bangladesh, Brunei Darussalam, Jordan, Kuwait, Lebanon, Qatar United Arab Emirates. Lebanon d. Qatar 3-0: T. Zahlan (LIB) d. S-K. Al-Alawi (QAT) 4–6 6–3 6–3; A. Hamadeh (LIB) d. N-G. Al-Khulaifi (QAT) 6–1 6–4; A. Hamadeh/Z. Hassan (LIB) d. M-S. Al-Khulaifi/N-G. Al-Khulaifi (QAT) 6–4 6–2. Kuwait d. Jordan 3-0: A. Al-Ashwak (KUW) d. F. Azzouni (JOR) 6–1 6–2; H. Al-Ashwak (KUW) d. L. Azzouni (JOR) 6–4 6–3; A. Abdul-Aziz/A. Al-Shatti (KUW) d. L. Azzouni/K. Naffa (JOR) 6–3 6–3. Bangladesh d. Brunei 3-0: S. Jamaly (BAN) d. I. Ibrahim (BRU) 6–1 6–3; H-L. Rahman (BAN) d. S. Dzulkiflee (BRU) 6–1 6–0; S. Jamaly/H-L. Rahman (BAN) d. N. Cheong/S-L. On (BRU) 6–1 6–0. Lebanon d. United Arab Emirates 3-0: B. Al-Munzer (LIB) d. O. Bahrouzyan (UAE) 6–3 6–4; A. Hamadeh (LIB) d. S. Al-Maktoum (UAE) 6–0 6–1; A. Hamadeh/Z. Hassan (LIB) d. O. Al-Ulama/H. Badri (UAE) 6–1 6–0. Kuwait d. Bangladesh 3-0: A. Al-Shatti (KUW) d. S. Jamaly (BAN) 6–1 6–1; H. Al-Ashwak (KUW) d. H-L. Rahman (BAN) 6–4 6–2; A. Abdul-Aziz/A. Al-Ashwak (KUW) d. S. Jamaly/H-L. Rahman (BAN) 6–3 7–6(4). Jordan d. Brunei 3-0: F. Azzouni (JOR) d. I. Ibrahim (BRU) 6–2 6–4; L. Azzouni (JOR) d. S. Dzulkiflee (BRU) 6–0 6–0; G. Hassan-Qadi/K. Naffa (JOR) d. N. Cheong/S-L. On (BRU) 6–1 6–4. Kuwait d. Brunei 3-0: A. Al-Shatti (KUW) d. N. Cheong (BRU) 6–0 6–0; H. Al-Ashwak (KUW) d. I. Ibrahim (BRU) 6–2 6–0; A. Abdul-Aziz/H. Al-Ashwak (KUW) d. N. Cheong/S-L. On (BRU) 6–0 6–0; Bangladesh d. United Arab Emirates 3-0: S. Jamaly (BAN) d. O. Al-Ulama (UAE) 6–0 6–3; H-L. Rahman (BAN) d. S. Al-Maktoum (UAE) 6–1 6–2; T. Hossain/D. Passia (BAN) d. H. Badri/O. Bahrouzyan (UAE) 6–2 6–0. Qatar d. Jordan 3-0: M-S. Al-Khulaifi (QAT) d. F. Azzouni (JOR) 6–7(5) 7–6(5) 6–3; N-G. Al-Khulaifi (QAT) d. L. Azzouni (JOR) 6–4 7–5; S-K. Al-Alawi/N-G. Al-Khulaifi (QAT) d. G. Hassan-Qadi/K. Naffa (JOR) 6–1 6–2. Lebanon d. Brunei 3-0: B. Al-Munzer (LIB) d. N. Cheong (BRU) 6–1 6–0; T. Zahlan (LIB) d. I. Ibrahim (BRU) 6–1 6–2; A. Hamadeh/Z. Hassan (LIB) d. N. Cheong/S-L. On (BRU) 6–2 6–0. Bangladesh d. Jordan 3-0: S. Jamaly (BAN) d. K. Naffa (JOR) 6–3 6–2; H-L. Rahman (BAN) d. L. Azzouni (JOR) 6–2 2–6 6–3; S. Jamaly/H-L. Rahman (BAN) d. F. Azzouni/L. Azzouni (JOR) 7–5 6–1. Qatar d. United Arab Emirates 3-0: M-A. Al-Saoud (QAT) d. O. Bahrouzyan (UAE) 6–3 6–1; N-G. Al-Khulaifi (QAT) d. S. Al-Maktoum (UAE) 6–0 6–1; S-K. Al-Alawi/M-S. Al-Khulaifi (QAT) d. O. Al-Ulama/H. Badri (UAE) 6–4 7–5. Lebanon d. Bangladesh 3-0: Z. Hassan (LIB) d. S. Jamaly (BAN) 6–3 6–1; A. Hamadeh (LIB) d. H-L. Rahman (BAN) 6–2 6–2; B. Al-Munzer/T. Zahlan (LIB) d. T. Hossain/D. Passia (BAN) 6–3 6–2. Kuwait d. Qatar 2-1: A. Al-Shatti (KUW) d. S-K. Al-Alawi (QAT) 6–0 6–2; H. Al-Ashwak (KUW) d. N-G. Al-Khulaifi (QAT) 6–4 7–6(4); S-K. Al-Alawi/M-S. Al-Khulaifi (QAT) d. A. Abdul-Aziz/A. Al-Ashwak (KUW) 0–0 ret. Brunei d. United Arab Emirates 2-1: O. Al-Ulama (UAE) d. N. Cheong (BRU) 2–6 6–7(5); I. Ibrahim (BRU) d. S. Al-Maktoum (UAE) 7–5 6–1 8-6; S. Dzulkiflee/I. Ibrahim (BRU) d. O. Al-Ulama/H. Badri (UAE) 6–4 6–3. Lebanon d. Kuwait 3-0: Z. Hassan (LIB) d. A. Al-Shatti (KUW) 6–2 6–2; A. Hamadeh (LIB) d. H. Al-Ashwak (KUW) 6–2 6–2; B. Al-Munzer/Z. Hassan (LIB) d. A. Abdul-Aziz/A. Al-Shatti (KUW) 6–4 6–3. Bangladesh d. Qatar 2-1: S. Jamaly (BAN) d. M-A. Al-Saoud (QAT) 6–1 6–0; H-L. Rahman (BAN) d. N-G. Al-Khulaifi (QAT) 4–6 6–0 7–5; S-K. Al-Alawi/N-G. Al-Khulaifi (QAT) d. T. Hossain/D. Passia (BAN) 3–6 0–6. Jordan d. United Arab Emirates 3-0: K. Naffa (JOR) d. O. Bahrouzyan (UAE) 6–4 6–1; L. Azzouni (JOR) d. S. Al-Maktoum (UAE) 6–4 6–4; F. Azzouni/L. Azzouni (JOR) d. H. Badri/O. Bahrouzyan (UAE) 6–3 6–1. Lebanon d. Jordan 2-1: B. Al-Munzer (LIB) d. G. Hassan-Qadi (JOR) 6–1 6–1; A. Hamadeh (LIB) d. K. Naffa (JOR) 6–1 6–1; G. Hassan-Qadi/K. Naffa (JOR) d. A. Hamadeh/T. Zahlan (LIB) 0–1 ret. Kuwait d. United Arab Emirates 3-0: A. Al-Ashwak (KUW) d. H. Badri (UAE) 6–0 6–1; A. Al-Shatti (KUW) d. O. Bahrouzyan (UAE) 6–1 6–1; H. Al-Ashwak/A. Al-Shatti (KUW) d. S. Al-Maktoum/O. Bahrouzyan (UAE) 6–2 6–1. Qatar d. Brunei 3-0: S-K. Al-Alawi (QAT) d. I. Ibrahim (BRU) 6–0 6–1; N-G. Al-Khulaifi (QAT) d. S. Dzulkiflee (BRU) 6–0 6–2; S-K. Al-Alawi/M-S. Al-Khulaifi (QAT) d. N. Cheong/S-L. On (BRU) 6–4 6–4. Lebanon were promoted to Asia/Oceania Group II for the 1997 competition. Jordan, Brunei Darussalam and United Arab Emirates were relegated to Group IV for the 1997 competition.

1st Round 9-11 February	Quarter-Final Round 5-7 April	Semi-Final Round 20-22 September	Final Round Nov 29-1 Dec

Russia

Italy 3-2

Italy

Italy 4-1

Austria

South Africa 3-2

South Africa

France 3-2

Germany

Germany 5-0

Switzerland

France 5-0

France

France 5-0

Denmark

India

India 3-2

Netherlands

Sweden 5-0

Belgium

Sweden 4-1

Sweden

Sweden 4-1

Hungary

Czech Republic 5-0

Czech Republic

Czech Republic 3-2

Mexico

USA 5-0

USA

**1996
Davis Cup
by NEC
World
Group**

FRANCE 3-2

CHAMPION NATION

Photography credits

Russ Adams: 52

Ron Angle: 30–1, 34, 35, 36–7

Clive Brunskill/Allsport: 50, 51, 53, 54–5, 68, 69, 70, 71, 72, 73, 75, 76, 84–5

Gianni Ciaccia/Sport Vision: 47, 58, 62, 74, 96, 97

Arne Forsell/Bildbyran: 46, 56, 78–9, 82, 83, 98, 99

Ingrid Gerencser/Gepa Pressefoto: 89, 92–3

Andrei Golovanov and Sergei Kivrin/Caviar Press: 87

Roger Gould: 32, 86

Rien Hokken: 57

Henk Koster: 42, 44–5, 48–9

Cristi Preda/Sport XXI: 90

Jean-Marc Pochat/Presse Sports: 77

Gary M. Prior/Allsport: 4–5, 7, 91

Angelo Tonelli: 33, 38, 39, 40, 41, 63, 64, 65, 94, 95, 100, 101

Paul Zimmer: 9, 14, 14–5, 16, 17, 18–9, 19, 20, 20–1, 22, 22–3, 24–5, 26–7, 27, 28–9, 43, 59, 60–1, 66–7,

80, 81, 102–3, 104, 105, 106, 107, 108, 109, 110, 111, 112, 113, 114, 115, 116, 117, 118, 119

Miguel Angel Zubiarrain: 88

Archive pictures in History of the Davis Cup chapter: Copyright of the Wimbledon Lawn Tennis Museum